JAMAICA KINCAID AS CRAFTER AND GRAFTER

JAMAICA KINCAID AS CRAFTER AND GRAFTER

Agency, Practice, Interventions

WAGADU VOL. 19

To order additional copies of this book, contact:
Xlibris
1-888-795-4274
www.Xlibris.com
Orders@Xlibris.com
547077

Editorial Team

Founding Editors
Mechthild Nagel, SUNY Cortland, United States
Nina Zimnik, Zürich University of Applied Sciences, Switzerland
Editor-in-Chief
Mechthild Nagel, SUNY Cortland
Managing Editor
Anne Adams, SUNY Cortland

Book Review Editor
Tushabe wa Tushabe, Kansas State University, United States
New Media Review Editor
Jean Young, University of Georgia-Athens, United States
Technical Advisory Team
Loren Leonard, SUNY Cortland
Assistant Editors at SUNY Cortland
Seth Nii Asumah, Africana Studies and Political Science
Lynn E. Macdonald, Physical Education
Andrew Fitz-Gibbon, Philosophy
Ibipo Johnston-Anumonwo, Geography
Brett Troyan, History
Nikolay Karkov, Philosophy

Linguistic Advisory Board
Thaddeus Blanchette, Federal University of Rio de Janeiro, Brazil
Hongli Fan, SUNY Cortland
Colleen Kattau, SUNY Cortland
Kassim Kone, SUNY Cortland
Paulo Quaglio, SUNY Cortland

Advisory Board
Carole Boyce Davies, Cornell University, United States
Fatima El-Tayeb, UC San Diego, United States
Ann Ferguson, University of Massachusetts-Amherst, United States

CONTENTS

FOREWORD

By Anne Adams, Managing Editor, Wagadu

This special issue of *Wagadu* results from a conference, *The Art and Craft of Grafting in Jamaica Kincaid's Works*, in spring of 2017, at the Sorbonne. Co-edited by Corinne Bigot, Andrée-Anne Kekeh-Dika, Nadia Setti, and Kerry-Jane Wallart, the articles in the volume explore various denotations and connotations of the notion of "grafting" in the Caribbean-American novelist's more recent works, specifically: *My Garden (Book):*; *Among Flowers: A Walk in the Himalaya*; and *See Now Then*, with connections also to Kincaid's earlier *The Autobiography of My Mother*.

With this volume, online, open-access *Wagadu: A Journal of Transnational Women's and Gender Studies* has again prepared a print version of Volume 19. Our mission is to engage feminist theory and practice in a postcolonial context. The journal is supported by the dedicated faculty and staff of the State University of New York, College at Cortland, USA. We continue to receive support from a diverse and international advisory and editorial board membership, making *Wagadu* one of the few notable open-access, postcolonial and feminist journals (online or in print). We thank Dr. Carlos Medina of the Office of Diversity, Inclusion and Equity of the State University of New York (SUNY), Dr. Erik Bitterbaum, President of SUNY Cortland, the William Haines Fund, and Université Paris 8 for funding the publication of this special issue.

We hope this volume will expand your thinking on the notion of "grafting" as the authors interpret it through the works of one of the most engaging contemporary women writers.

Wagadu: What's in a Name?

Wagadu—the Soninke name of the Ghana Empire—controlled the present-day Mali, Mauritania and Senegal and was famous for its prosperity and power from approximately 300-1076. It constituted the bridge between North Africa, the Mediterranean and Middle Eastern worlds and Southern Africa. Ghana gave birth to the two most powerful West African Empires: Mali and Songhay. The modern country of Ghana (former British Gold Coast) derives its name from the Ghana Empire.

Legend says that Ghana's power derived from a mythic python, which generated the rich gold deposits and controlled the fortunes of the empire. Year after year the people of Ghana had to offer the most beautiful virgin to the python as a sacrifice. One year, the distressed fiancé of a sacrificial girl took a sword and beheaded the mythic python in a preemptive move. The head flew and crashed into the parts of West Africa that became gold producing regions leading to the rise of the Mali Empire. Ghana fell after seven years of drought and poverty forced the Ghana people, the Soninke, to disperse and adopt exodus as a way of life to this day.

Why Wagadu? Wagadu has come to be the symbol of the sacrifice women continue to make for a better world. Wagadu has become the metaphor for the role of women in the family, community, country, and planet. The excerpt below from a Soninke song best summarizes this state of fact:

> *Duna taka siro no yagare npale*
> *The world does not go without women.*

Wagadu, Journal of Transnational Women's and Gender Studies
Special Issue: Jamaica Kincaid (2018)

EDITORIAL

JAMAICA KINCAID AS CRAFTER AND GRAFTER: AGENCY, PRACTICE, INTERVENTIONS

Guest Editors:
Corinne Bigot, Toulouse Jean Jaurès University
Andrée-Anne Kekeh-Dika, University Paris 8
Nadia Setti, University Paris 8
Kerry-Jane Wallart, Sorbonne University

Contact:
Corinne Bigot, Toulouse Jean Jaurès University; Andrée-Anne Kekeh-Dika, University Paris 8; Nadia Setti, University Paris 8; Kerry-Jane Wallart, Sorbonne University
corinne.bigot@wanadoo.fr; andree-anne.kekeh-dika@univ-paris8.fr; nadia.setti@univ-paris8.fr; kjwallart@yahoo.fr
To cite this editorial:
["Editorial." *Wagadu: A Journal of Transnational Women's and Gender Studies,* Summer 2018, vol. 19, pp. 1-5]

> In the beginning was my word and my word became the
> world as I ordered it to be. If it now sounds too bold,
> if it now sounds too made up, if it now sounds too in
> retrospect, all the same it is true. (*Talk Stories, 11)*

Jamaica Kincaid's provocative statement in her introduction to *Talk Stories* lays blunt claim to the singularity of her own "word" even as she self-consciously reprocesses the Bible. Excessive as it may sound, Kincaid's statement captures and recasts her unabashed positioning as regards the issues of filiations and debts which traverse her production at large. Also at stake here is Kincaid's engagement with an imaginative and theoretical construct of what women's Caribbean writing might be all about—the rehabilitation of the "true," of the primacy of personal experience as a legitimate and valuable point of departure towards creation (Tate, 1985, p. xvii; Boyce Davies & Savory Fido, 1990, p. ix). The writer's abrupt formula forcibly gestures toward what Kincaid actually does with writing, *i.e.*, "taking positions and changing words" as Cheryl Wall has it (Wall, 1989, pp. 1-15), "making up" with different materials, tinkering with, grafting, and disrupting the foundation and certainties of dominant and less dominant languages and frames. Indeed, in the beginning is Kincaid's word, in the ways she estranges vernacular, ordinary language as well as scientific discourses. She makes them radically other as she extensively reworks existing genres and texts (her own included), stocks of clichés and images in order to forge idiosyncratic ways of inscribing her multiple Caribbean selves in the global cultural landscape (see Boyce Davies on "portable identities," 2013, p. 53). Kincaid's makeshift writing takes much in its stride, as she crafts and grafts ordinary material into her textual fabric – books of all sorts, tools, plants and fruits, food, weeds, photographs, garment, craftwork, popular culture iconic texts, artefacts and songs, among many others. The writer takes it all, recycles this deceptively ordinary material, opening up in turn unexpected venues into classical music or Greek mythology, and entering intertextual conversations with scientists, writers and thinkers across the world.

Writer Michelle Cliff, for one, has touched on the grafting image, the mango, as a way of rendering the versatility of the Caribbean: "In Jamaica we are as common as ticks. / We graft the Bombay onto the common mango. The Valencia onto the Seville. We mix tangerines and oranges. We create mules." (Cliff, 1985, p. 22). This issue suggests that Jamaica Kincaid goes one step further as she expands and extends the grafting process into creative practice / praxis and ways of stretching the horizons of words. This, she does through deliberate but unauthorized incursions into scientific domains as she proceeds to explicit or implicit deliberations with writers and creative artists the world over – Colette, Vita Sackville-West, Tsitsi Dangaremgba, Henry James, Michel Butor, Bruno Schulz, or film-maker Pat Barker (Kekeh-Dika, 2016). Grafting and crafting her writing way, Kincaid's work moves on in a deceptively "disorderly" fashion (Kincaid, 2001, p. 222) and finds new entries into the familiar, as Jamie Herd shows in her contribution to this issue. Kincaid's move toward discursive genres (autobiographical, fictional, essayistic) is one more example of the ways in which the practices of grafting and crafting may help elucidate her writing venture. Grafting is an apt image for the capacity of her writing to change texture and direction, to overlap and complicate boundaries and connections of all sorts, as with her "Wisteria" (Kincaid, 1999, pp. 11-28).

Jamaica Kincaid's words, "I use a cut and slash policy," in her interview with Gerhard Dilger (1992, pp. 21-25) imply a rough and concrete type of approach to words. They also highlight Kincaid's desire to associate her writing enterprise with the ordinary manual practices her personae are engaged in—sewing, knitting, gardening, and cooking among other things. Cutting and slashing adequately account for the painful labor of the author's writing hand, of forcing words out of their usual route and trying to put them back together; of possibly reviving language, bodies, garments or plants through seeing them from a new perspective. As she cuts and slashes, Kincaid also recycles images often used to account for female creativity (knitting, sewing, quilting, as shown by Woolf [1927], Walker [1983], Kingsolver [2013]) distorting them, rearranging or estranging them along the way. The volume seeks to explore Kincaid's "policy of writing," which we understand as her political and aesthetical commitment to the word. The articles presented here scrutinize her urge to cut and trim, to get rid of what is unnecessary or overused, as well as the desire to expand what needs expanding, or perhaps repeating, to borrow from Benítez-Rojo's theorizing of repetition as a fundamental mode of Caribbean creativity (Benítez-Rojo, 2001). In the beginning was Kincaid's words; her constant arrangement and "worrying" (Williams, 1979) her own words and others' demonstrate that in order to move beyond boundaries one needs to go back one step and move on again.

Jamaica Kincaid has been a household name in the United States and in the Caribbean for a long time now and much has been written about her works there and, more recently so, in Europe (Boyce Davis, 1994; Ferguson, 1994; Brooks Bouson, 2005; Donatien-Yssa, 2007; Braziel, 2009; Yassine Diab, 2014; Kekeh-Dika, 2016). This volume is timely in its taking stock of the resonances of grafting in Kincaid's later texts, looking back and ahead at the same time, scrutinizing new "relational readings" (Wall, 1991, p. 9) of Kincaid's writings. One of the points of departure of this volume was the conference on Jamaica Kincaid's works co-organized by Université Paris 8 (Saint-Denis), Université Paris Sorbonne and Université Toulouse Jean Jaurès in May 2017, "The art and craft of grafting in Jamaica Kincaid's works." The conference endeavored to put to the fore how the notion of graft can be understood and articulated from diverse points of entry (botany, craftsmanship, and text-building). The authors explore in this issue how grafting, seen as painful historical reminder and as clinical, agricultural and textual practice, operates in Kincaid and helps approach her more recent production. The volume focuses on the writer's latest books, which have been less examined by scholarly inquiry: *See Now Then* (2013), *Among Flowers: A Walk in the Himalaya* (2005), and *My Garden (Book):* (1999). A number of contributions also connect these publications with *The Autobiography of My Mother* (1996), notably through the ways in which this particular novel introduces "domesticating/ed" practices (see Alexander).

The volume evidences how the clustered notions of art, graft and craft make fuller sense of the many branches, rootstocks and fragments of Kincaid's world as they initiate a critical dialogue with unexpected domains, but also as they draw the outlines of a metafictional reflection on writing. Through their focuses on Kincaid's refashioning missing links, bodies, filiations, women's gardens, provision grounds and other submerged subtexts, the contributors lay special emphasis on Kincaid's skillful invention and fabrication of replacements; they pay heed to how she grafts together spare parts of the self and kin into textual fragments that recompose what has been lost in life stories and collective History. These articles thus put to the fore how the everyday, gardening, botanical practices address Kincaid's critical and literary enterprise, her ways of revisiting established narratives and of encroaching onto History and science (botany in particular) in order to envision other ways of (re) defining a writer's own positional and critical praxis.

This volume of *Wagadu* is comprised of eight diverse inquiries into how grafting functions as a metaphor for seeing and writing the world. Carole Boyce Davies foregrounds the tensions springing from a (doubly) diasporic Caribbean identity; after Fanon, she connects the dots between displacement and dislocation, between spatial containment and transformational experiences. Her forays into Kincaid's distinct positionality, both as an insider and an outsider, shed light upon the expansive, fluid and migratory nature of Caribbean spaces. Boyce Davies convincingly underpins the overlapping areas present in such novels as *Lucy* and *Annie John*, but also *Among Flowers*, whose reflection on tourism is a case-in-point of Kincaid's ambivalent politics.

Jamie Herd looks at Kincaid's latest novel, *See Now Then*, and juggles its generic singularity and indeterminacy with Gérard Genette's notions of hypertextuality and parody; she traces the webs of semantics and semiotics radiating from a text where "[t]he madwoman in the attic has been recast as a madwriter with a voice, a garden, a set of knitting needles and a room all her own." Herd demonstrates how thinking of writing in terms of grafting reveals practices that, for all their resistance to conciliatory solutions, aim at repairing damage and resisting disease: the original purpose of botanical grafts, after all.

The diasporic dimension of Jamaica Kincaid's œuvre is at the core of Myriam Moïse's essay, as she yokes together *My Garden (Book):* and Olive Senior's *Gardening in the Tropics*. In both literary texts the garden generates unexpected processes of memory. Moïse demonstrates how such processes go hand in hand with the construction of spaces as unstable categories; in the wake of Ben Heller she interrogates the links between female subjectivity and landscape and shows that transculturalism is not merely about transgressing borders but about leaving linearity behind.

Pauline Amy de la Bretèque posits the similarities and asymmetries between grafting and creolization; her paper embraces both the historical context of the plantation and the role of botany in the economy of colonial territories, as well as the proposals of recent investigations in ecopoetic criticism in the field of Caribbean Studies by such critics as Savory (2011), Braziel (2005), DeLoughrey, Gosson and Handley (2005). This article also scrutinizes how Kincaid pays attention to the scientific names of plants, in a postcolonial revisiting of language that functions as an endless process of (perhaps impossible) epanorthosis, or "redressing."

In a paper centered around Kincaid's "gardening books," Josette Spartacus addresses the ambivalences of gardening, of shaping the ground, mapping out a territory, and possessing plants, in the context of the post-plantation and through the concept of Benítez-Rojo's meta-machine. This repeating machine, which projects its pattern on plants but also on writing, is that of the conquest itself, Spartacus argues.

In the continuity of Marden's "plant thinking," Eleanor Byrne follows the meandering of two plants which have been endowed by Kincaid with a series of significations and even more so, with a sense of evasiveness and unreadability: the wisteria and the rubber tree. Such an emphasis on moments of epistemological appropriation is in keeping with DeLoughrey's insistence that ecocriticism, which has been devised around discussions on North American literature, cannot be borrowed straightforwardly and applied to Caribbean literature. Byrne moves on to isolate moments in Kincaid's *My Garden (Book):* when "the ghosts of the individual life, of the personal story suddenly open into the history of the world itself."

Natacha D'Orlando tackles issues of biopower as she sees emerging in *The Autobiography of My Mother* a possible metaphor of the child as a graft, through master discourses on genealogy echoing back to the biological practices inherited from the colonial period. Through the gendered perspective of Caroline Rody's "mother-as-history" concept, D'Orlando sheds light on the complex handling of the narrator's body in this novel; a body whose self-creation also unleashes a fair deal of destruction outside itself, as the recurrent abortion motif intimates.

In a paper also focused on *The Autobiography of My Mother* Simone Alexander takes up a slightly different route as she addresses the botanical possibilities in terms of disrupting and reactivating linearity and lineage and considers the human implications of such lines. Alexander's scrutiny of the novel's sexual exploitation and suspended genealogies leads her to ponder on the tension between visibility and invisibility; this in turn convokes the figure of the ghost and makes for a prism through which to envisage the very concept of the timeline.

All contributions in this issue tackle dynamics of self-awareness and processes of liberation as they are introduced by Kincaid through a myriad of practices. Stock forms of text mediality are grafted onto rhizomic explorations and interpellations, writing back to what Young had identified as "the threat of the fecund fertility of the colonial desiring machine" (1995, p. 166). Kincaid's "archi-textures" (Sheller, p. 209) resonate here with the most up-to-date research in such fields as ecocriticism, trauma studies, affect studies, diaspora studies and transculturalism and form a welcome addition to critical interventions around the Antiguan writer's more recent work.

References

Benítez-Rojo, A. (2001). *The Repeating Island. The Caribbean and the Postmodern Perspective.* (J.E Maraniss, Trans.). Second Edition. Durham, NC and London: Duke University Press. (Original work published 1989)

Boyce Davies, C. & Savory Fido E. (Eds). (1990). *Out of the Kumbla: Caribbean Women and Literature.* Trenton, NJ: Africa World Press.

Boyce Davies, C. (2013). *Caribbean Spaces: Escapes from Twilight Zones.* Champaign, IL: University of Illinois Press.

Braziel Evans, J. (2009). *Caribbean Genesis. Jamaica Kincaid and the Writing of New Worlds.* Albany, NY: SUNY Press.

Brooks Bouson J. (2005). *Jamaica Kincaid: Writing Memory, Writing Back to the Mother.* Albany, NY: State University of New York Press.

DeLoughrey, E., Gosson R., & Handley G. (Eds.). (2005). *Literature and the Environment: Between Nature and Culture.* Charlottesville, VA: University of Virginia Press.

Cliff, M. (1985). *The Land of Look Behind.* Ithaca, NY: Firebrand Books.

Donatien Yssa, P. (2007). *L'Exorcisme de la blès, vaincre la souffrance dans L'autobiographie de ma mère de Jamaica Kincaid.* Paris : le Manuscrit.

Kekeh-Dika, A-A. (2016). *L'imaginaire de Jamaica Kincaid : Variations autour d'une île caraïbe*. Pessac: Presses Universitaires de Bordeaux.

Kincaid, J. (1992). I Use a Cut and Slash Policy of Writing, Jamaica Kincaid Talks to Gerhard Dilger. *Wasafiri, 16*, 21-25.

Kincaid, J. (1999). *My Garden (Book):*. New York, NY: Farrar, Straus and Giroux.

Kincaid, J. (2001). *Talk Stories*. New York, NY: Farrar, Straus and Giroux.

Kingsolver, B. (2013). Where it Begins. *Orion Magazine*. Retrieved from https://orionmagazine.org/article/where-it-begins.

Sheller, M. (2012). *Citizenship from Below: Erotic Agency and Caribbean Freedom*. Durham, NC: Duke University Press.

Tate, C. (Ed.) (1985). *Black Women Writers at Work*. New York, NY: Continuum.

Wall, C. (Ed). (1989). *Changing our Own Words. Essays on Criticism, Theory, and Writing by Black Women*. New Brunswick, NJ: Rutgers University Press.

Williams, S. A. (1979). The Blues Roots of Contemporary Afro-American Poetry. In M. S. Harper and R. B. Stepto (Eds.), *Chant of Saints. A Gathering of Afro-American Literature, Art, and Scholarship* (pp.123-135). Urbana, IL: University of Illinois Press.

Yassine-Diab, N. (2014). *Aliénation et réinvention dans l'oeuvre de Jamaica Kincaid*. Montpellier : Presses universitaires de la Méditerranée.

Young, R. (1995). *Colonial Desire: Hybridity in Culture, Theory and Race*. London: Routledge.

TWO

JAMAICA KINCAID, CARIBBEAN SPACE AND LIVING DISLOCATIONS

Carole Boyce Davies
Cornell University

Contact:
Carole Boyce Davies, Cornell University
ceb278@cornell.edu

To cite this article:

[Carole Boyce Davies. "Jamaica Kincaid, Caribbean Space and Living Dislocations." *Wagadu*: *A Journal of Transnational Women's and Gender Studies*, Summer 2018, vol. 19, pp. 6-25]

Abstract

This essay brings together two recent intellectual concerns: The first the core of my *Caribbean Spaces* (2013) which defined Caribbean Space as encompassing island spaces, the circum-Caribbean and the Caribbean diaspora. The second, "Dislocations and Diaspora" which puts the statistical reality of increasing millions of displaced people in conversation with the earlier critical theories of displacement. I argue that these are also areas of intense engagement in the writings of Jamaica Kincaid.

> On that day, completely dislocated, unable to be abroad with the other, the white man, who unmercifully imprisoned me, I took myself far off from my own presence, far indeed, and made myself an object. (Fanon)
>
> My relationship to the Caribbean was one of dislocation, of displacement, literally or figuratively (Stuart Hall)
>
> I am in a state of constant discomfort and I like this state so much I would like to share it. (Jamaica Kincaid)

For this essay[i] I thought it would be useful to bring together two of my most recent intellectual concerns: one the core of my most recent book *Caribbean Spaces* (2013) and the second a recent paper I did on "Dislocations and Diaspora" for a conference on The Politics of Location in Manchester, UK. In the former, I was deliberately working with an expanded definition of Caribbean Space as encompassing island spaces, the circum-Caribbean and the Caribbean diaspora within a range of theories on space and place. The latter was a study which brought together actual human displacement as revealed in UNHCR *Global Trends,*[ii] in order to allow the statistical reality of increasing millions of displaced people to be read against or with the earlier critical theories of displacement. I see both of these (Caribbean Spaces and human displacement) coming together in the writings of Jamaica Kincaid.

Looking back over the body of work contributed by this writer, I see four or five overlapping tendencies operating:

- The family/autobiographical narrative
- The critique of European colonialism – its antecedent, coloniality, and continuing permutations arising with Western modernity
- The reading of Caribbean "small space" political, cultural and social practices and systems including the critique of tourism
- The impetus for and implications of the conditions of migration
- The Creole Garden/Private Garden vs Colonial botanic experiments.

I should say as well, prefatorily, that returning to Kincaid's work, I am amazed, but not surprised, by the amassing of a vast bibliography on all aspects of this writer, way beyond the first tentative essays included in *Out of the Kumbla. Caribbean Women and Literature* (1990). There, the single essay by then-grad student Giovanna Covi, "Jamaica Kincaid and the Resistance to Canons," actually foreshadowed a body of writing on what was seen then as perhaps the most experimental writer in a new generation of writers. My own essay for that collection, "Writing Home: Gender and Heritage in the Works of Afro-Caribbean/American Women Writers" actually addressed the issue of psychological dislocation in *Annie John* in particular as the girl seeks to identify herself first in relation to and then subsequently in opposition to her mother (p. 65).

A stark increase in literary attention to Caribbean women writers was the intent of conferences of the Association of Caribbean Women Writers and Scholars, designed precisely for the purpose of providing a body of critical writing on the growing number of Caribbean women writers. Recent literary companions to Kincaid's work such as Lizabeth Paravisini-Gebert, *Jamaica Kincaid: A Critical Companion* (1999) and more recently Mary Ellen Snodgrass's *Jamaica Kincaid. A Literary Companion* (2008) provide good overviews of the scholarship on and scholarly themes which have engaged critics of this writer.

Single-authored texts and numerous essays and, of course, individual conferences on her work indicate the extent to which Jamaica Kincaid has achieved the level of attention that most writers desire.

In the first epigraph to this paper, taken from *Black Skin, White Masks*, Franz Fanon talked about the dislocation he felt as a black man in relation to the way he was/is racially interpellated by the white world and its racial constructions:

> On that day, completely dislocated, unable to be abroad with the other, the white man, who unmercifully imprisoned me, I took myself far off from my own presence, far indeed, and made myself an object. (p. 112)

In "The Lived Experience of Blackness," Fanon works through the various processes of objectification, still ending though with the famous waiting for himself as the discussion ends: "I wait for me. In the interval, just before the film starts, I wait for me" (p. 140). Perhaps he should have read Hurston's "How it Feels to be Colored Me" and that classic line: "No I do not weep at the world. I am too busy sharpening my oyster knife" (p. 153). It would take Fanon several years to find himself through that inherited dislocation in what he defines as "the corporeal schema," ending with his determination to question everything. And it would come through a hard critique of colonialism and his own commitment to activism as a response.

I want to suggest at the outset that Jamaica Kincaid's entire self-articulation, represented well by the third epigraph, is more along the lines of the fighting back of a Zora Neale Hurston. Hers is an assertive response, as she experiences dislocation within family; within her community; in relation to Caribbean colonial manners; in her small place Caribbean landscape; but also subsequently as a black woman from the Caribbean living in a world which already constructs one in a particular set of narratives; and above all as a creative artist. Her response is always to return the gaze, re-narrativize the experience. She is not waiting for herself to appear as early Fanon does. She unfolds the self through multiple avenues. I want to suggest also that she embraces this dislocation in much the way that the Hall epigraph suggests but takes it a step further. So, let us examine what some of these dislocations and the ability to "take space," which is a hallmark of Caribbean cultural self-presentation, mean in three movements:

I. Kincaid's Rejection of Spatial Containment

At the end of the magical *At the Bottom of the River*, there is a wonderfully evocative construction of a world that our author sees/imagines, in which nature is alive with beauty and transformation. But there is also a self in which the conjunction of land and sea is transformational: "I looked at this world as it revealed itself to me—how new, how new—and I longed to go there" (p. 78). Clearly a re-fashioning of a limited world, to an imagined world with a parallel quest for an elsewhere, fundamental to diaspora, fundamental to the creative artist. This, it seems to me, is what typifies the entire journey of Jamaica Kincaid and captures the dissatisfaction she feels with enforced containment to smallness and the inability for many to see or imagine beyond specific localities. Hers, then, is a rejection of spatial confinement and a desire for a consistently expanding space—an argument I also make in *Caribbean Spaces*.

In many ways, my work as a scholar of Caribbean origin who migrated to the United States for educational advancement occupies the same temporal and geographical spaces as does Kincaid's. As such, her process is fully intelligible to me, as it is also the experience of friends and family. Coming of age as colonialism ended and new nations began to work out themselves in the Caribbean without resources, migration loomed consistently as the pathway to a more advanced life experience. We know from recent works like Hilary Beckles's *Britain's Black Debt. Reparations for Slavery and Native Genocide* (2013) and the discourse of Caribbean reparations this story: three-to-four hundred years of slavery and extractive colonialism left the Caribbean with little in terms of institutions, infrastructure and resources, except with the open possibility of migration to Europe for some, to North America for others, as one way of accessing education or getting back some of those economic resources. But we also know that those migrations, in either context, did not necessarily produce uniformly the promises of "a better life" or the full belonging that was often assumed on departure. This takes us back to the Fanon example above or Selvon's *Lonely Londoners* or Donald Hinds's *Journey to an Illusion* narratives for the UK. The US then was more hopeful than it is today for the activism and promise of challenges to racial subordination by Civil Rights/Black Power movements, ushered in new possibilities, ironically being curtailed under a president who in his campaign and election in 2016, created explicit white nationalist alliances. For many of us now this is another realization of that difficult location of migration—being displaced from home but also displaced in this new location. This reminds us that dislocation was/is, we can conclude, always a parallel experience of that diaspora creation.

Examining the trajectory of diaspora and migration discourses in order to situate our discussion we can say briefly that while the discourse of diaspora has become a popular academic consideration in the late 20th century and into the 21st century, the histories of transatlantic slavery and forced migration and the consequent diaspora creation have always remained significantly central to the definitions of black subjectivity in the Americas. Kincaid explores these well in *Annie John* (1983), particularly in the section on "Columbus in Chains" in which Annie is punished for offering a critique of false discovery, European domination and colonialism. In other portions of that text she provides the girl's angle on colonial schooling geared to constructing compliant natives, and clearly she would not be one of those. By the time we get to *A Small Place* (1988), we are fully into a heightened critique of the entire process of the collaborative exploitation of the Caribbean by a variety of world powers.

I develop some of these issues more fully in previous work but there are two relevant essays I want to identify, largely because they were co-written with a political economist and therefore are delicately balanced between literary and cultural analysis and actual socio-economic data: "Imperial Geographies and Caribbean Nationalism: At the Border between a Dying Colonialism and US Hegemony" (*New Centennial Review*, 2003) and "Migrations, Diasporas, Nations: The Re-making of Caribbean Identities" (2009).[iii] The argument in the latter was that the Caribbean navigates between the longer historical diaspora and the more recent Caribbean Diaspora created in the pre- and post-independence migrations; and in the former, that we are caught between contending colonial/imperial impulses.

In this context, Caribbean political and intellectual identity have moved consistently towards a critique of that difficult legacy of slavery and its related structural inequalities and the ongoing oppression created by extractive colonialism and its aftermath, which created intra-migrations and also precipitated new migrations and diasporas.

It is important to say here that in my *Migrations of the Subject* published in 1994, I signaled the beginning of a certain set of inquiries on migration. Still, it was a theoretical contribution more directly to discourses of subjectivity—arguing that the subject has migratory capability depending on a range of factors—age, race, place, geography, national identity, language, sexuality and so on. In many ways, Jamaica Kincaid's work, which up until then included *At the Bottom of the River* (1978), *Annie John* (1985), *Lucy* (1990), and *A Small Place* (1988), would be highly illustrative of my arguments. Generally, I have found her work as always providing amazing confirmations and additional revelations that were missing in the largely male corpus of literature of the writers developed in London, still writing back to empire. For example, she is one of the first to offer an intense detailing of North American migration. And when she does do England, as in "On Seeing England for the First Time," it is a scathing critique of all that hyped and perfect seat of empire. Much as it did for the character Antoinette/Bertha in Jean Rhys's *Wide Sargasso Sea*, England fell short and was therefore way less than what was created in the colonial imagination. Some called this essay bitter or angry. But Audre Lorde and Kincaid have great responses to that charge, insisting always on the creative use of anger.

Still, Jamaica Kincaid never idealizes or accepts idyllic Caribbean narratives uncritically. In fact, as *A Small Place* shows, she rejects almost everything that had negatively shaped this Caribbean home place and its people: colonization, corrupt neo-colonial politics, neglect, pettiness. But it is the rejection and hard critique of a critical insider/outsider, who sees with an eye for detail the many idiosyncrasies, anomalies and perversions wrought on a Caribbean slave society and their legacy on today's people.

Significantly as well, we have perhaps for the first time, the exploration of sexuality in a context in which Caribbean literary masculinity had prevailed for so long. Thus "the relationships between girls as they encounter Caribbean worlds" (Boyce Davies, 1994, p. 125)— the Red Girl, of course, and wildness and perhaps the first statement of another possibility of love: "Now I am a girl, but one day I will marry a woman—a red skin woman with Black bramble bush hair and brown eyes, who wears skirts that are so big I can easily bury my head in them" (Kincaid, 1992, p. 11). Sensuous writing in every way and, also critical of all those colonial manners and the ways that the mothers sought to enforce these is captured marvelously and succinctly in "Girl."

Once migrated, one sees in the representative *Lucy* (1990) of 1960s and 1970s generation, a critical thinker who can write almost anthropologically about the white family with which she works as the writer herself moves from au pair girl to writer and becomes in some ways representative of the generation of women who would strike out from the Caribbean, as her character does at the end of the novel *Annie John* (1985), determined to make a life abroad for themselves. And it is urban and suburban New York, sexuality and family life that concern her, tracing the pathway of the Caribbean migrating subject.

But here it is important to jump ahead to *Talk Stories* (2001), because, although published together as a group, they represent the microscopic detail that became her hallmark and which both provided the minutiae of American living and set the tone for subsequent writing. Here we see a kind of reverse anthropology with which she studies the idiosyncrasies of North American domestic and public life between 1974 and 1983. It is significant that the first talk story is on the Brooklyn carnival called Labor Day and which she titles "West Indian Weekend." The exportation of Caribbean carnivals we know has become one of the prime signifiers in the claiming of expanding Caribbean Spaces, and Jamaica Kincaid documents this in the *New Yorker*. Along the way in detailing this New York it is almost like having a lab at her disposal, as she encounters a range of popular culture figures and we witness that meticulous cataloging of American follies, waste and excess.

Interspersed throughout is her own self-writing, and identification of important elements in the Caribbean cultural history and manners, the remnants of plantation culture: "The Ground" (Kincaid, 2001, p. 88), for example, is the same "Provision Grounds" that Sylvia Wynter describes as fundamental to the creation of African belonging in the Caribbean landscape. And here the leap:

> I grew up on an island in the West Indies which has an area of a hundred and eight square miles. On the island were many sugarcane fields and a sugar making factory and a factory where both white and dark rum were made. There were cotton fields, but there were not as many cotton fields as there were sugar cane fields. There were arrowroot fields and tobacco fields, too, but there were not as many arrowroot fields as there were cotton fields. Some of the fifty-four thousand people who lived on the island grew bananas and mangoes and eddoes and dasheen and christophine and sweet potatoes and white potatoes and plums and guavas and grapes and papaws and limes and lemons and oranges

and grapefruits, and every Saturday they would bring
them to the market which was on Market street and
they would sell the things they had grown. ... I now live
in Manhattan. The only thing it has in common with
the island where I grew up is a geographical definition
(Kincaid, 2001, pp. 87-91).

After that, she proceeds to talk (definitely shortsightedly) about the
difference in sleeping hours and the absence of the necessity for most
people on an urban island to awake early to make a living from selling
produce under difficult farm to market conditions. It is shortsighted
because there are many laborers who work as early as do Caribbean
farmers, in order to prepare the city streets, and public transportation
for the masses who will traverse them.

Stuart Hall, as we have indicated, concluded that "dislocation and
disjuncture" are fundamental to being located in diaspora. But that
same dislocation and disjuncture also marked his experience of being at
home…in other words both embody versions of dislocation, particularly
for the non-conforming individual. This is perhaps what Kincaid
articulates best. For both Fanon and Hall describe a double or triple
dislocation but also, particularly for Hall, an assumption of dislocation
perhaps which is fundamental to the modern human condition. CLR
James had already argued that Caribbean subjects are among the earliest
to experience this modern condition of displacement and dislocation.
Dislocation is also a hallmark of the modern condition.

II. Living Dislocation and Diaspora

My more recent project defined *Caribbean Spaces* beyond the limitations
to islands, seas and ocean scapes, and it evoked Guyanese writer Wilson
Harris's *The Womb of Space*, in which he described concentric horizons
to talk about space in more advanced ways. I was also fascinated by the
idea of circulations of ideas, people, cultural forms, politics rather than
simply diasporic movement from one location to the other, but a series

of circulations of people in a kind of desire for a global relation or world space. In other words, the vision was not for me simply Atlanticist but a Caribbean Space that is recognizable beyond the Atlantic, a kind of larger unbounded mobile Caribbean trans-nation.

The assumption of a series of homes, then, is what is suggested for the Caribbean diasporic activist, whether it is a Fanon or a Claudia Jones; but also for everyday people. Caribbean identity, according to Dionne Brand, is one which has to be ready for continuous self-invention. "After the *Door of No Return,* a map was only a set of impossibilities, a set of changing locations … A map, then, is only a life of conversations about a forgotten list of irretrievable selves," Dionne Brand says repeatedly in her work by that name (p. 224).

The logic of circulations, I argued in *Caribbean Spaces*, captures best the spatially-expanding movements of people, ideas, politics, cultural forms that come from the Caribbean and circulate internationally through a series of global migratory processes which continued throughout the 20th century to create new identities and parallel histories. These identities—sexual, religious, ethnic, class, gender—operate tectonically. Still, as I have argued before, beyond the theoretics of post-colonialism, we need new vocabularies that describe the various encounters between the different 'worlds' ushered in by a variety of forces.

So, what are some of these issues of location and dis/location particularly for the modern subject? In "Other Tongues. Gender, Language, Sexuality and the Politics of Location," the final chapter of *Migrations of the Subject,* I argued the following, which still actually works now:

> The politics of location brings forward a whole host of identifications and associations around concepts of place, placement; location, dis-location; memberment, dis-memberment; citizenship, alienness; boundaries, barriers, transportations; peripheries, cores and centers. It is about positionality in geographic, historical, social,

economic, educational terms. It is about positionality in society based on class, gender, sexuality, age, income. It is also about relationality and the ways in which one is able to access, mediate or reposition oneself, or pass into other spaces given certain other circumstances. (p. 153)

Diaspora, then, carries with it always a sense of "dislocation" or removal from any sense of fixity in a given location. And for those living in the now defined Caribbean Diaspora, this **double dislocation** is captured in the historical but ongoing movement of peoples, first from originary geographic and cultural fields (Africa, India etc.) and then the subsequent economically-generated movements to the centers of colonial-administrative policy in the British sense (Hall) but later to the North American context. The distant homeland (say, Africa or India or China) recedes further into the realm of ancestral memory and the imaginary; the more recent homeland, also a site of dislocation, is then layered onto that meaning.

Historians can demonstrate that similar movements have taken place in the past, with time and place providing additional markers of migration. Thus, Hall was able to use his location in Britain, himself doubly or triply diasporized, to comment on this developing phenomenon: "My relationship to the Caribbean was one of dislocation, of displacement, literally or figuratively," he says (p. 272). In other words, a colonized subject is already dislocated, already spoken for in someone else's terms, subjected then and therefore always, then migrating to the "centre" (physically or emotionally) of that same colonizing world which had already displaced you to be further displaced or dislocated both from home and from the people and conditions around one (p. 272). Here is Hall's prophetic conclusion to what is perhaps his final major essay:

The disruption of people from their settled places, from their homes, from their familiar surroundings, their roots in the land and landscape, from their traditional ways of life, from their religions, from their familial

> connections – the uprooting has become the history of
> modern "global" society … The fact of the homeless, of
> people who only survive by buying a ticket from some
> person who is trading in bodies, hanging out on the
> bottom of a train, crossing boundaries at the depth of
> night, running the gauntlet of surveillance cameras and
> border controls and disappearing into the depths of the
> cities. The economic migrants and the asylum seekers, the
> illegal immigrants, the *'sans papiers'* — the ones without
> proper papers. The ones driven into the camps across the
> borders by famine, civil war, environmental devastation
> or pandemic … We were the forerunners. (p. 287)

So, in this view, there is always a dark side or the "underbelly of the
contemporary globalization system." But note also that, for Hall, it is
out of that dislocation and displacement that something new emerges.
For the Caribbean intellectual, the geography of the fragmented island
or archipelagoes and their relation to the sea has been a conduit and
repository for histories and becomes a consistent trope for Caribbean
writers: Benítez-Rojo's historico-economic sea; Walcott's socio-historical
sea; Brathwaite's "tidalectics"; Glissant's archipelagization. Interesting
readings such as Edwidge Danticat's "Children of the Sea" which
actually takes one into the boat itself capturing in two voices the
separation, pain, loss and impending doom for those who take on the
sea as precarious escape—the boat about to be engulfed by the sea itself.

III. Landed: The Creole Garden/Private Garden and the Colonial Botanist

But let us try to land then, and finally, landed, let us come back to and
simultaneously go forward to, the Private Garden. Even as she creates
a garden and writes *My Garden (Book):* (1999) in Vermont, the author
realizes that her garden "resembled a map of the Caribbean and the
sea that surrounds it … I only marveled at the way the garden is for
me an exercise in memory, a way of remembering my own immediate

past, a way of getting to a past that is my own (the Caribbean Sea) and the past, as it is indirectly related to me (the conquest of Mexico and its surroundings)" (p. 8). And even here, as she details and critiques some aspects of American culture, the past intervenes, as she compares her present house with the house she grew up in and the assorted punishments associated with that era of Caribbean parenting (p. 44). Kincaid admits that, much as she detested the work and meanings of her mother's Creole Garden, it nevertheless has influenced her own "private garden." In fact, the entire gardening experience, we learn, is an attempt to bring riotous Caribbean color into the otherwise winter white and seemingly dead landscapes of Vermont:

> It is winter and so my garden does not exist; in its place
> are these mounds of white, the raised beds covered with
> snow, like a graveyard, but not a graveyard in New
> England, with its orderliness and neatness and sense of
> that's-that, but more like a graveyard in a place where
> I am from, a warm place where the grave is topped
> off with a huge mound of loose earth, because death
> is just another way of being ... The snow covers the
> ground in the garden with the determination of death,
> an unyielding grip, and the whiteness of it is an eraser,
> so that I am almost in a state of disbelief (p. 69).

She contrasts this winter garden with color in the Caribbean and her garden in its bloom, a certain kind of creative disorder and definitely color. In an interesting essay titled "Mobility and Anxious Cosmopolitanism: Jamaica Kincaid's *Among Flowers*," scholar Pramod Nayar describes Kincaid's travel in search of seeds with a botanist in the Himalayas as exhibiting a dual neocolonial travel paradigm: "simultaneously abrogating the cultural authority to control and name which the colonial traveler embodied as well as the 'individualized leisure travel of the privileged Black First worlder here.' It is significant that her travel is under the auspices of National Geographic but it is also an experience of displacement ... a kind of disorientation in space" (p.7). He cites another essay by Zoran

Pecic, "Floral Diaspora in Jamaica Kincaid's Travel Writing" which also concludes that "The ambiguity of being aware of her own colonial legacy of exploitation and gardening and her sense of dislocation and alienation … locates her in an uncanny space between the familiar role of gardener and the unfamiliar position of world traveler" (p. 11).

My sense is that this dislocation is precisely familiar space for Kincaid, a kind of ultimate dislocation which the essay gets at:

> Her anxiety resides in the forced detachments he practices and exhibits from all her legacies: as Caribbean (with its fraught history of plantation and slavery), as a diasporic migrant in the USA with its history of racism, as a First Worlder embarked on a journey to a Third World region where the two regions are connected in an iniquitous relationship. (Nayar, p. 11)

A similar essay is Jeanne Ewert's "Great Plant Appropriators and Acquisitive Gardeners: Jamaica Kincaid's Ambivalent *Garden (Book)*:" in *Jamaica Kincaid and Caribbean Double Crossings* (2006), which comments on Jamaica's travels to China and to various other locations in Europe precisely to get seeds of exotic plants for her garden suggesting that Kincaid had "joined the class of botanical explorers and conquerors" (p. 117). She concludes after all that Kincaid is in some ways re-enacting transplantation, "the unhomeliness of the de-territorialized subject" (p. 123).

For her part, Jamaica Kincaid is well able to make these distinctions in terms of her own migrating subject position and the possibility of more than one identity or subject position in operation. In an interview with Marina Warner "Among Flowers: Jamaica Kincaid in Conversation," published in *Wasafiri* 21:2 (2006) she says:

> … the book I wrote about tourism was talking about
> the continued exploitation of a group of people, but
> in this other form. Now was I exploiting, was I an

> eco-tourist, a new concept? Usually the tourist seems to
> go somewhere and have a good time, generally speaking.
> I don't think there is much of a good time to be had by
> a botanist-tourist in this part of the world. (p. 56)

In a journey which carried a level of pain, including having to remove leeches, difficult bridges and unending hiking, we have again the series of overlapping locations I want to suggest between the kind of Creole Garden/Private Garden that her mother cultivated, the Provision Grounds that African people in the Americas cultivated during and following plantation slavery to make a living and the ability of a Caribbean girl to finally have enough resources to acquire beautiful flowers, to visit another location in search of beauty or whatever exists there, to search for the horizon as Hurston also did. All of these desires had been launched by that imagined world we began with from *At the Bottom of the River*.

Sylvia Wynter has interesting discussions about Provision Grounds, planting and cultivating not for profit but for putting one's markers in an environment as providing the basis for the indigenization of Africans into the Caribbean landscape, which I include in an essay "From Masquerade to Maskarade. Caribbean Cultural Resistance and the Re-humanizing Project" (2015). We can also read Jamaica's Vermont garden as her own expansion of Caribbean Space; her own creation of a grounded space, if you will, and with the same impetus as West Indian Weekend—to create a certain chaos and insertion of color in otherwise bleak and uninviting North American and European landscapes.

The power imbalance between the colonial botanist with the imperative to rename, possess and control everything and a Jamaica Kincaid trying to understand the world has no symmetry. The power, of course, was evident/is still evident in the same system that she has critiqued in the ways that the colonials labeled everything, moved things, people and plants around the world, created different landscapes for profit and control.

An interesting contrast is that today at "Farm to Plate" conferences—one held recently in the heart of the Finger Lakes (May 11-13, 2017), others in other locations in the U.S.—people describe the need for food security, encourage gardening for sustenance and survival and beauty in urban locations and comment on the absence of the black gardener even in more progressively liberal communities.

In "Imperial Geographies and Caribbean Nationalism" we had argued that anti-colonial agency has for a long time remained the exclusive property of the black male who remained culturally bound to Europe in time and place. For Kincaid, it is always the tension between the drives of encapsulation into small places and drives of transcendence; safety and willful travel pushing the boundaries of the possible, that permeate her version of Caribbean discourse. For Kincaid, then, dislocation and its discomforts at every level possible remain always:

> I am in a state of constant discomfort and I like this state
> so much I would like to share it. (Kincaid, 1999, p. 229)

But also

> How bound up I am to all that is human endeavor, to
> all that is past and to all that shall be, to all that shall
> be lost and leave no trace. (Kincaid, 1992, p. 82)

References

Beckles, H. (2012). *Britain's Black Debt. Reparations for Slavery and Native Genocide.* Mona, Jamaica: University of the West Indies Press.

Benítez, Rojo, A. (1992). *The Repeating Island. The Caribbean and the Postmodern Perspective.* (J.E. Maraniss, Trans.) Durham, NC: Duke University Press.

Boyce Davies, C. (1990). Writing Home: Gender and Heritage in the Works of Afro-Caribbean/American Women Writers. In C. Boyce Davies and E. Savory Fido (Eds.), *Out of the Kumbla. Women and Literature* (pp. 59-73). Trenton, NJ: Africa World Press.

Boyce Davies, C. (1994). *Black Women, Writing and Identity. Migrations of the Subject.* London: Routledge.

Boyce Davies, C. (2013). *Caribbean Spaces. Escape Routes from Twilight Zones.* Urbana Champaign, IL: University of Illinois Press.

Boyce Davies, C. (2015). From Masquerade to Maskarade. Caribbean Cultural Resistance and the Re-humanizing Project. In K. Mc Kittrick (ed.), *Sylvia Wynter. On Being Human as Praxis* (pp. 203-225). Durham, NC: Duke University Press.

Boyce Davies, C. & Jardine, M. (2003). Imperial Geographies and Caribbean Nationalism: At the Border between a Dying Colonialism and US Hegemony. *New Centennial Review: 3*(3), 151-174.

Boyce Davies, C. & Jardine, M. (2009). Migrations, Diasporas, Nations: The Re-making of Caribbean Identities. In C. Mohanty and M. Wetherell (Eds.) *Sage Handbook of Identities* (pp. 437-454). London: Sage Publications.

Brand, Dionne. (2001). *A Map to the Door of No Return.* Toronto: Vintage (Random House).

Covi, Giovanna. (1990). Jamaica Kincaid and the Resistance to Canons. In C. Boyce Davies and E. Savory Fido (Eds.), *Out of the Kumbla. Caribbean Women and Literature* (pp. 345-354). Trenton NJ: Africa World Press

Danticat, E. (1995). Children of the Sea. In Danticat, E. *Krik? Krak!* (pp. 1-30). New York, NY: Soho.

Ewert, J. (2006). Great Plant Appropriators and Acquisitive Gardeners: Jamaica Kincaid's Ambivalent Garden (Book). In L. Lang-Peralta, *Jamaica Kincaid and Caribbean Double Crossings* (pp. 113-126). Newark: University of Delaware Press.

Fanon, F. (1967). *Black Skin, White Masks.* New York, NY: Grove Press.

Glissant, E. (1999). *Caribbean Discourse.* Charlottesville, VA: University of Virginia Press.

Hall, S. (1999). Thinking the Diaspora: Home Thoughts from Abroad. *Small Axe, 6,* 1-18.

Hall, S. (2007). Thinking About Thinking. In S. Hall, *Caribbean Reasonings: Culture, Politics, Race and Diaspora: The Thought of Stuart Hall.* Kingston, Jamaica: Ian Randle.

Harris, W. (1983). *The Womb of Space. The Cross-Cultural Imagination.* Westport, Conn.: Greenwood Press.

Hinds, D. (1966). *Journey to an Illusion. The West Indian in Britain.* London: Heinemann.

Hurston, Z. N. (1979). How it Feels to be Colored Me (1928). In A. Walker (Ed.), *I Love Myself When I'm Laughing,* (pp. 152-155). New York, NY: The Feminist Press.

Kincaid, J. (1985). *Annie John.* New York, NY: Farrar, Straus and Giroux.

Kincaid, J. (1988). *A Small Place.* New York, NY. Farrar, Straus and Giroux.

Kincaid, J. (1990). *Lucy.* New York, NY: Farrar, Straus and Giroux.

Kincaid, J. (1992). *At the Bottom of the River.* New York, NY: Farrar, Straus and Giroux. (First published 1978).

Kincaid, J. (1999). *My Garden (Book):.* New York, NY: Farrar, Straus and Giroux.

Kincaid, J. (2001). *Talk Stories.* New York, NY: Farrar, Straus and Giroux.

Kincaid, J. (2007). *Among Flowers. A Walk in the Himalaya. National Geographic.*

Nayar, P. (2013). Mobility and Anxious Cosmopolitanism: Jamaica Kincaid's *Among Flowers. Transnational Literature* 6 (1).

Paravisini-Gebert, L. (1999). *Jamaica Kincaid: A Critical Companion.* Westport, CT: Greenwood Press.

Pecic, Z. (2010). Floral Diaspora in Jamaica Kincaid's Travel Writing. In J. D. Edwards and R. Graulund (Eds.), *Postcolonial Travel Writing: Critical Explorations* (pp. 138-155). Basingstoke: Palgrave Macmillan.

Rhys, J. (1966). *Wide Sargasso Sea*. New York, NY: W.W. Norton.

Selvon, S. (2006). *The Lonely Londoners*. London: Penguin. (First published 1956).

Snodgrass, M. E. (2008). *Jamaica Kincaid. A Literary Companion*. Jefferson, NC: Mc. Farland.

Warner, M. (2006). Among Flowers: Jamaica Kincaid in Conversation. *Wasafiri 21*(2), 52-57.

Wynter, S. (1970). Jonkonnu in Jamaica: Towards the Interpretation of Folk Dance as a Cultural Process. *Jamaica Journal* 4(2), 34-48.

THREE

ROOTSTOCK OR SCION:
GRAFTING RADICAL DIFFERENCE
IN JAMAICA KINCAID'S
SEE NOW THEN

Jamie Herd
Université Paris 8

Contact: Jamie Herd, Université Paris 8
jamie_herd75@yahoo.fr
To cite this article:
[Jamie Herd. "Rootstock or Scion: Grafting Radical Difference in Jamaica Kincaid's *See Now Then*." *Wagadu: A Journal of Transnational Women's and Gender Studies*, Summer 2018, vol. 19, pp. 26-42]

Abstract

Through the paradigm of grafting, this article examines intertextual and generic complexities in Jamaica Kincaid's *See Now Then.* It considers how the author produces literary and subjective nourishment by harnessing anger as a creative force while offering up one form of resistance to the bad life.

Published as a novel in 2013, the non-linear narrative *See Now Then* portrays the birth and eventual disintegration of the Sweet family. Reviewers immediately seized upon autobiographical elements (names, roles, places, events) of the work, pigeonholing the book as thinly disguised vengeance for the author's real-life divorce, a tale of "hell-hath-no-fury-like-a-woman-scorned." In interviews with *The American Reader* and *Guernica*, Jamaica Kincaid dismissed these readings for their lack of critical substance and leveled charges of racism against critics who qualified the novel (and, indeed, the body of her work) primarily as "angry" (see Alleyne, 2013 and Loh, n.d.). "People only say I'm angry because I'm black and I'm a woman," Kincaid told *The American Reader* (Loh, n.d., para. 14), questioning why white authors escape the labels "angry" and "autobiographical." At the risk of contradicting the novelist, I would argue that the reviewers were correct to pick up on anger in *See Now Then* (and other works), for each of the family members harbors anger towards the others. These initial readers nonetheless failed to do justice to the author's aesthetic and ethical use of anger, intentionally sidestepping critical engagement with a longstanding tradition of women's (auto)fiction. I'll argue here that, like Kincaid's previous works, *See Now Then* harnesses and redirects anger as a creative force by using complex intertextual and generic grafting to demand truths be told *and* heard.

Grafting in the Novel Garden

For Kincaid, writing and gardening are interconnected. "Even when I'm not writing, *I'm writing*—often while I'm weeding my *garden*," she confided in a 1990 interview with *Harper's Bazaar* (as cited in Bouson, 2005, p. 190). Seven years later, recounting her brother's dying and death, she equated writing with personal survival in *My Brother* (Kincaid, 1997, pp. 195-196). In keeping with this dual vision of writing as gardening and writing as survival, I would like to associate reading and gardening through the paradigm of grafting. In the garden, the scions of prized fruit varieties are selected and adapted for fruit propagation, combining the need for sustenance with the will for pleasure. Viewed in this way, Kincaid's writing emerges as a form of both subjective and literary nourishment in which literary grafting is used to propagate fruits on which to survive, but also on which to thrive. The secret to thriving lies in the diversity of fruits produced as well as in the capacity of the garden or the novel to sustain health. I'll use R. J. Garner's *The Grafter's Handbook*, an authoritative reference on plant grafting for gardeners and agriculturalists since 1947,[iv] to guide my thinking on how diversity is achieved in *See Now Then* and to comment upon some of the novel's generic and intertextual complexities and their meanings.

In a short glossary, *The Grafter's Handbook* defines the verb *graft* as follows: "to prepare and place together plant parts so that they may grow together" (Garner, 2013, p. 24). Yet the seeming simplicity of this definition is undermined from the first chapter of the manual, "Grafting in Nature and Antiquity," which explains that certain plants growing in close proximity may join together "naturally," i.e. without assistance from human hands. Affirming that grafting with detached scions can be traced back to the earliest gardens of Mesopotamia, the author is left to speculate that early grafters learned their craft from plants themselves: "It seems reasonable to suppose that artificial grafting followed upon observation of natural grafting . . . " (Garner, 2013, p. 36). Grafting is then an in-between craft (neither "natural" nor "artificial," between occurrence and practice) for liminal, productive spaces, such as novels[v] and gardens.

Gerard Genette (1997) affirms this in *Palimpsests* when he writes: "Hypertextuality refers to any relationship uniting a text B (which I shall call *hypertext*) to an earlier text A (I shall, of course, call it the *hypotext*), upon which it is grafted in a manner that is not that of commentary" (p. 5). Like a scion grafted onto rootstock, the hypertext must bear its own fruit in the new, liminal space of the text. I'd now like to consider Genette's definition alongside a passage from *The Grafter's Handbook* explaining the reasons for grafting:

Plants may be grafted in a multitude of ways and for many different reasons. The art may be exercised merely as a pastime, but grafting is usually employed to gain one or more of the following objectives:

1. To propagate, or to assist in propagating, plant varieties not otherwise conveniently propagated.
2. To substitute one part of a plant for another.
3. To join plants each selected for special properties, e.g. disease resistance or adaptability to special conditions of soil or climate.
4. To repair damage, to overcome stock/scion incompatibility, and to invigorate weakly plants.
5. To enable one root system to support more than a single variety or one branch system to derive from more than one root system.
6. To elucidate problems of structure, growth, and disease. (Garner, 2013, p. 28)

Through intertextual and intergeneric grafting, *See Now Then* achieves similar aims. Inspired by Kincaid and Genette, I've reworked the excerpt from the manual for literary purposes (in bold) to make this clear:

Texts may be **g/crafted** in a multitude of ways and for many different reasons. The art may be exercised merely as a pastime, but **textual g/crafting** is usually employed to gain one or more of the following objectives:

1. To propagate, or to assist in propagating, **textual** varieties not otherwise conveniently propagated.
2. To substitute one part of a **text** for another.

3. To join **texts** each selected for special properties, e.g. disease resistance or adaptability to special conditions of **cultural** soil or climate.
4. To repair damage, to overcome **hypotext/hypertext** incompatibility, and to invigorate weakly **texts**.
5. To enable one **cultural root** system to support more than a single **textual** variety or one **cultural** branch system to derive from more than one **cultural** root system.
6. To elucidate problems of structure, growth, and disease.

As with Genette's classifications of transtextual relationships, these reasons to graft overlap and intersect.

Propagating Multiple Shoots

The parallel between botanical and literary grafting is apparent early in the novel, with Jamaica Sweet—writer, dutiful wife and mother—portrayed lying in the Shirley Jackson house, surrounded by seed catalogues, the *Iliad* and *The Library of Greek Mythology*. She is both bereaved by the death of the much-loved handyman, Homer, and beleaguered by conflicts between her son Heracles and his father, Mr. Sweet, a composer who disdains taking his son bowling in the city of Troy. While the athletic and hyperactive Heracles spends a great deal of time in the garden playing with plastic Myrmidons from McDonalds, his sister Persephone is often stolen away by her father for music lessons, much to the distress of Mrs. Sweet, a modern-day Demeter, who mopes about daughterless in her garden. But the life Mrs. Sweet leads is not one of conflict and grieving alone. There is also time to socialize and laugh with neighbors like Cadmus and Harmony Arctic. These references to Greek mythology and literature illustrate how Kincaid simultaneously calls on and calls into question the Western literary canon, using ancient texts as rootstock for the novel. But in *See Now Then*, she topworks the familiar old tree, that is to say, she shears off its branches and grafts the remaining structure with multiple scions.

The seed catalogues mentioned earlier make up just one group of the many textual scions embedded into the novel's rootstock. Jamaica Sweet's bedtime readings to her children splice in numerous English-language children's classics, including titles like *Goodnight Moon* (1947) and *The Runaway Bunny* (1942) by Margaret Wise Brown and *Where the Wild Things Are* (1963) by Maurice Sendak. It is, of course, worth noting that the wild things are not so much wild as cultivated within the liminal garden-novel space. Of particular interest are the rabbits, described in the novel as "rodent[s] much loved by children and hated by anyone with an unfenced vegetable garden" (Kincaid, 2013, p. 134). In this passage as in others, Beatrix Potter's Peter Rabbit scampers through the diegetic space (I shall return to Potter later in this article), crisscrossing the paths of the oddly anthropomorphized rabbits of *Goodnight Moon* and *The Runaway Bunny*. In the latter, mother rabbit pursues baby bunny in a series of mutations that end in a becoming human, before the bunny decides it would be just as easy to remain a rabbit than to try and outwit the rather overbearing mother rabbit. Grafted into Kincaid's novel, these titles appear as more recent shoots of ancient myths and literature in which metamorphoses and family drama raise questions as to what it means to be human. As these scions bind themselves to the novel's rootstock, they act to breakdown the cloister that would separate high literature from children's literature, showing them to be compatible in "nature."

Reader and writer Jamaica Sweet is also passionate about cooking, consulting and commenting upon a wide variety of recipes. Tellingly, the names of the authors—Marcella Hazan, Paula Peck, Elizabeth David, Edna Lewis, and Nika Hazelton—or unmistakable references to their person—Julia Child, rather than the titles of the cookbooks—appear in the text. Implicitly, these cookbooks send out new, productive growth from the stock, and a clear connection is made between reading, writing and nourishment, confusing the literal and metaphorical meanings of the term.

Calling attention to these writers, exclusively women and all cultural icons, elevates women's culinary contributions as worthy of cultural or literary attention, highlighting all the while the often unsung role women play in providing nourishment to their families and communities. Marcella Hazan transmitted Italian cooking traditions to English-speaking audiences (see Sipress, 2013), while Nika Hazelton shaped thinking about food across North America (see O'Neill, 1992). Edna Lewis, interestingly, was also a restaurateur whose Café Nicholson was frequented by celebrities and a dressmaker who copied designer creations for the New York elite. She was known for her own African-inspired creations (see Lam, 2015). Calling on Lewis and her cornbread recipe through Jamaica Sweet, Kincaid indirectly conjures up her own short story, "Biography of a Dress," published in 1992, in which a yellow cotton poplin dress for a two-year old child is compared to yellow cornmeal. The story establishes clear linkages between what is available to eat, making the dress, and the family's economic situation: "But I was then (not so now) extremely particular about what I would eat, not knowing then (but I do now) of shortages and abundance, having no consciousness of the idea of rich and poor (but I know now that we were poor then) … " (Kincaid, 1992, para. 1). The familiar temporal adverbs "now" and "then" are evidence that Kincaid is connecting *See Now Then* to earlier writings through an investigation of time that spans the body of her work

Several references to works from "then" have been embedded into the "now" of *See Now Then*. For example, Mr. Sweet is described as hating Mrs. Sweet entirely, "especially her enthusiasms," which included "growing species of rare flowers from seeds she had gone hunting for in temperate Asia" (Kincaid, 2013, p. 92), a reference to Kincaid's travel narratives, *Among Flowers: A Walk in the Himalaya* (2005) and *My Garden (Book):* (1999). "The Dean and Mrs. Hess," published as a short story in 2011 in *Little Star*, has been fully integrated into the novel. Though told to Heracles as a bedtime story, within the greater context of *See Now Then*, the story reads much like a geological creation myth, bringing us back to Kincaid's claim that "Eden is never far from the gardener's mind. It is the Garden to which we all refer, whether we know it or not" (Kincaid, 2005, p. 189). Deceivingly familiar passages from Jamaica Sweet's writing (Kincaid, 2013, pp. 28-32, pp. 166-167, pp. 176-178) that read like excerpts from *Annie John* (1983), *Lucy* (1990), *The Autobiography of My Mother* (1996) or *Mr. Potter* (2002) also appear between quotation marks but are "imitations." The first of these "false" citations, which describes a character we presume to be the young Mrs. Sweet, recounts how a young girl's mother gives birth to her a second time by teaching her to read in the public library in Saint John's, Antigua (Kincaid, 2013, pp. 30-32). This could be the library immortalized in *A Small Place* (1981) or it could be a reworking of scenes from Kincaid's other works. It might also be a grafting device used to connect *See Now Then* to other Caribbean women's narratives. Mrs. Sweet's depiction resonates strongly with Audre Lorde's (1982) biomythographical recollection of her own coming to literacy, a rebirth that came when the young, visually-impaired author first acquired glasses (Lorde, 1982, pp. 21-25). After all, in Mrs. Sweet's words, the precocious girl who, like Lorde, knew how to read before she went to school "could see things within the book that [she] was not meant to see …" (Kincaid, 2013, p. 31). Furthermore, by seeing things both then and now, Kincaid, akin to Lorde, "challenges that split between writer and theorist" (Boyce Davies, 1994, p. 54). Kincaid's scions disseminate textual varieties that are not easily propagated within the literary establishment. Whatever the author's reasons may be, these are pastiche shoots for parodic rootstock.

Hear, Hear: Telling it Like it Was

Therefore, when Genette seeks to define parody in *Palimpsests*, there is a very familiar ring to his words: "First, the etymology: *ode*, that is the chant; *para*, "along," "beside." *Parodein*, whence *parodia*, would (therefore?) mean singing beside, that is, singing off key; or singing in another voice—in counterpoint; or again, singing in another key—deforming, therefore, or *transposing* a melody" (Genette, 1997, p. 10). The novel has been cleverly orchestrated, taking on the characteristics of an experimental composition, with the voices of the Sweet family members responding to one another, almost simultaneously telling the family tale. When composer Mr. Sweet is not silently berating his spouse for her loud, verbal *faux pas* (Kincaid, 2013, pp. 170-171), he is lamenting Jamaica Sweet's singing, which is often off key (p. 86). Described as growing up in the era of Lord Executor, the Mighty Sparrow and other calypso stars, the fictional novelist belts out old Motown hits, recites rap lyrics from Outcast and Eminem and sings folks tunes from her native island to her children. Mrs. Sweet's musical repertoire is firmly rooted in the traditions of the African diasporas of the Americas, cueing readers into the harmonies and counter-discourses of modernity that Paul Gilroy (1993) designated as forming the Black Atlantic.

But though Jamaica Kincaid has deftly grafted popular musical intertexts from African-American and Caribbean traditions onto literary rootstock, she has also embedded her work with classical music references from European and Russian traditions, from the Baroque period to the 20th century, with a particular focus on atonal music. This works to undermine the hierarchy dividing "popular" and "serious" music. Mr. Sweet plays the music of Dmitri Shostakovitch,[vi] is sought out by his student-turned-lover for his thoughts on Arnold Schoenberg's *Pierrot Lunaire* and is equally praised for his knowledge of Igor Stravinsky and Alban Berg. This body of twentieth century composers of atonal music also reveals much about Kincaid's grafting process.

Atonal music is organized around patterns and references to previous compositions rather than a tonal center or key (see "Atonal," 2017). Like Schoenberg's *Pierrot Lunaire,* the novel is written in free counterpoint, playing with known literary forms and shifting from the perspective of one family member to that of another as the marriage disintegrates. Mr. Sweet busies himself composing a series of nocturnes on the theme of a dead marriage and is distracted by the "sound of the washing machine washing the clothes of his infernal family" (Kincaid, 2013, p. 21), which becomes the "dunning sound caused by the washing machine and the clothes dryer and the hub-hub of the household beyond" (p. 22), and is later rearranged and extended to "the spinning of the washing machine and then the sharp whir of the clothes dryer, and doors banging shut, not in anger but thoughtlessness, and the screams of the children from pain or pleasure, and that bitch singing" (p. 164). An incident in which Mrs. Sweet fails to pick her children up from the bus stop on time is also repeated, in varying detail (Kincaid, 2013, pp. 127-135; p. 166), and Heracles sees through his father's hypocritical epitaph, referring to Mrs. Sweet as "my beautiful wife," in at least two passages (p. 99; p. 162).

The playfulness of these (re)arrangements is not, however, purely a matter of pleasure or intergeneric grafting. *See Now Then* also makes rather explicit reference to and use of serialism, a method of composition initially developed by Schoenberg and adopted by students "… in which a fixed permutation, or series, of elements is referential … Most commonly the elements arranged in the series are the 12 notes of the equal-tempered scale" (Griffiths, 2017). Persephone sings out the contents of the Delia's catalogue to her mother and brother:

> Her voice at the same twelve pitch and then in a row
> that might be familiar and then unexpectedly not, or
> so it seemed to poor, benighted Mrs. Sweet's ears …
> how cruel to make you love one thing twelve times and
> then change to something else and make you love that
> and then change to something else and make you love
> that too and then make the thing you loved new and
> not tell you and then you love that too and then change
> to something you had forgotten and make you love
> that too and then change to something you know and
> loved then and love now and make you think you don't
> know it at all. … [S]he thought that the twelve pitches
> arranged in a row and then repeated over and over again
> and then changed unexpectedly might be as beautiful
> as trees arranged in rows of five diagonally placed

and evenly spaced and therefore called a quincunx ...
(Kincaid, 2013, pp. 133-134)

This passage brings another prominent emotion of the narrative, love, into focus and links trees and the arrangement of trees (something between "nature" and "nurture") to musical composition.

Kincaid uses serialism to tune references to atonal music into the history of slavery and colonialism and to continue her career-long critique of the Enlightenment project. This is perhaps most evident in the repetitious recollection of Mr. Sweet's jab at Mrs. Sweet (Kincaid, 2013, p. 23; p.77; p. 122; p. 125):

> ... Mr. Sweet had said to her that she looked like the actor Charles Laughton when he portrayed the captain of a ship, sailing from the South Pacific with a cargo of saplings, in which the crew mutinied. Mrs. Sweet knew the movie very well, for the cargo of the ship at the time the crew mutinied was the breadfruit, a staple of Mrs. Sweet's diet when she had been a child, and it had been a staple of the diet of children born for generations before hers and all those children hated this food. (p. 74)

Mr. Sweet's comment may have been tongue-in-cheek, and *See Now Then* certainly metes out ample and often below-the-belt criticism of his physical appearance, comparing him at one point to a Mesozoic rat (Kincaid, 2013, p. 24), and of his upper crust upbringing. But like the "ships in motion" Paul Gilroy (1993) chose as the "organizing symbol" for his study of the black Atlantic (p. 4), the Mutiny, set sail anew in *See Now Then,* and the breadfruit issue an imperative to remember, an imperative to tell truths about how and why trees travelled, about the fruits trees bear and about what eating them means.

Hence, though Persephone's mother is said to have "untutored and Third World-attuned ears" (Kincaid, 2013, p. 134), the telescoping of

Mrs. Sweet and Jamaica Kincaid makes a mockery of the slight. She instead shows herself to be a master grafter set on embedding multiple fruit-bearing shoots into the rootstock of *See Now Then*, watching the intertextual and intergeneric grafts disrupt time as they branch out in new directions. For the grafter plays with time, making old trees bear new fruits and young rootstock grow scions of fruit-bearing trees of the past. Beholding the grafted tree is seeing time defied, at once seeing now then and seeing then now.

Repairing Damage: from Grafting to Crafting

In addition to propagating textual varieties to bear diverse fruits, *See Now Then* also uses grafting to repair damage. This demonstrates that in the novel, like the garden, grafting "is the healing in common of wounds" (R. J. Garner, 2013, p. 33), a way to recover and sustain health. In *My Brother*, Kincaid portrayed her writings as an attempt to restore beloved books tossed into the fire by her mother: "... it would not be so strange if I spent the rest of my life trying to bring those books back to my life by writing them again and again until they were perfect, unscathed by fire of any kind" (Kincaid, 1997, pp. 197-198). *See Now Then* emerges as yet another hypertext of the writer's dearly departed copy of *Jane Eyre* (1847), a reworking of Charlotte Brontë's Caribbean wife, a spouse betrayed by her wealthy, cultured and, in this most recent rendering, American husband. In the words of Mr. Sweet:

> ... I don't love your mother anymore, I love another woman who comes from somewhere else, another woman with whom I have been talking about ballroom-dancing lessons and we talk about Mozart ... I don't love your mother, you know, we were always so incompatible, for she did emerge from a boat whose main cargo was bananas, and she is strange and should live in the attic of a house that burns down, though I don't want her to be in it when that happens, but if she was in it when

the house burned down, I wouldn't be surprised, she is
that kind of person. (p. 159)

However, the destinies of the novel's spouses have also been altered to
fit new purposes. The madwoman in the attic has been recast as a mad
writer with a voice, a garden, a set of knitting needles and a room all
her own "where she communes with the world before 1492" (p. 145).
There, she sits thinking of and through her Antiguan mother, much
to the chagrin and mockery of Persephone, Heracles and Mr. Sweet.
With a pen for secateurs, Jamaica Sweet, like Jamaica Kincaid, grafts
her own tales onto old and ancient literary rootstock, and one might
muse as to whether or not Woolf would have taken Kincaid's writing
to task, as she did Brönte's. Would she, like the initial reviewers of *See
Now Then*, have called out some supposedly false note in Kincaid's
writing, accusing the novelist of "writi[ng] of herself when she should
be writ[ing] of her characters" (Woolf, 1989, p. 70)? Or, does Kincaid's
literary crafting ring true to Woolf's definition of literary integrity, that
is to say, as conveying the conviction of truth (Woolf, 1989, p. 72)?

Readers familiar with non-fiction works like *My Garden (Book):* and
Among Flowers might recognize the writer cloaked in Mrs. Sweet, eating
oranges in a hot bath to fight off the New England winter or admiring
the neighbor's peonies. A famous photo of Kincaid from her early days
at *The New Yorker* might be called to their mind's eye when Mr. Sweet
recollects his wife's

> … naturally black hair, thick and coarse as ropes that were
> usually found in the hands of stevedores, cut off so short
> that she might be mistaken for a stevedore himself, the
> color of her hair was the color of new rope in the hands of
> a stevedore—blonde; her eyebrows removed with a razor
> and in their place a line drawn in … colors …" (p. 88)

As parody, *See Now Then* reads against *My Garden (Book):* and *Among Flowers* almost like, taking Genette's lead once again, a "… text, preserved but turned inside out like a glove." (Kincaid, 2013, p. 14).,

However, no one-to-one correspondence should be made between Kincaid and Mrs. Sweet, an avid knitter who darns the family's socks and creates tunics for Heracles. This reminds us that grafting is also an old synonym of knitting ("Grafting, n.", 2017, 3.d.), which speaks to the historical co-development of food cultivation and textile production for clothing (see Mazoyer & Roudart, 2006). As humans mastered the art of agriculture, they produced more and more textiles from the plants and animals they raised. And so, the same Mrs. Sweet who grieves her daughter like Demeter, who uses dressmaker Edna Lewis' recipe for cornbread (Kincaid, 2013, p. 63) and who wears "a lovely brown dress made by *Lilith*" (p. 179, my emphasis), also knits, purls and drops stitches, weaving literary and mythological threads into "the garment that had been her own life" (p. 164).

> [T]he hem of this garment had become undone, … and from time to time it made her trip over her own self … the hem needs to be mended thought poor Mrs. Sweet, the hem needs to be made more secure, for the elbows and knees and forehead, these were just the parts that were visible, all the parts of her that the unraveling garment caused to be bruised could not be seen … .
> (pp. 164-165)

Perhaps this unraveling of her life is what inspires Mrs. Sweet to take up the task of knitting an Aran sweater, like those worn by Irish sailors of the Aran Islands, another of the world's small places. This image is particularly fitting, for the novel and for the body of Kincaid's work, as the stitching of the Aran sweater was said to be family-specific, allowing loved ones to identify deceased sailors washed ashore by their sweaters (Mayorga, 2014, pp. 15-16). This brings to mind another meaning of grafting—the ornamental weavings of nautical ropes ("Grafting", n.,

2017, 3.a.), and another critical metaphor, that of writing as a craft (i.e., an art and a small boat). In her analysis of Olive Senior's *Gardening in the Tropics*, Alison Donnell offers up this smaller, lightweight boat as an alternative to Paul Gilroy's chronotope of ship, one better suited to understanding how Senior's and, more generally, Caribbean women's writing (Donnell, 2005, pp. 94-104) navigate the cultural waters of the Black Atlantic.

As the representations of Mrs. Sweet knitting multiply, so do her doubles. At times, she appears as Demeter or as a fictionalized Kincaid. At others, she might bear a closer resemblance to Arachne, weaving a tapestry portraying less flattering stories of her family and less savory moments in history. Perhaps she is one of the Fates, spinning the thread of life at arbitrary lengths and deciding when a life's time is up. Or might the crafty grafter be more of a trickster, a master of disguises? The numerous references to writer Beatrix Potter certainly suggest as much. The Englishwoman's characters were, of course, inspired by the African-American folktales of Brer Rabbit compiled by Richard Chase and retold by Joel Chandler Harris in 1855 in *The Complete Tales of Uncle Remus* (Harris, 1983). This rich folklore, which originated in West Africa, is a shared heritage of the African diasporas of the Americas, with stories taking various twists and turns in their migrations (see Walker, 2001). Might Mrs. Sweet then be an Aunt Nancy—half-woman, half-spider—hiding just out of site (see "Brother Rabbit doesn't Go to See Aunt Nancy" in Chandler Harris, 1995, pp. 865-867)? Shanna Greene Benjamin (2005), who spotted Aunt Nancy in the "web and weaving imagery" (p. 51) of Paule Marshall's (1983) *Praisesong for the Widow*,[vii] explains,

> During the Middle Passage, however, Ghanaian Ananse experiences a "sea change" that altered not only his name, but also his function in diasporic society. In Ghana, he was a "creative culture hero" while in Jamaica (and other parts of the Caribbean) he became a "trickster-par-excellence". In the United States, he becomes

> she: Aunt Nancy the healer, the master mediator, and
> revolutionary transitional life force. … Half woman and
> half spider Aunt Nancy's physical hybridization typifies
> the ideological doubleness particular to her depiction in
> nineteenth—and early—twentieth-century literature
> as she who mends the mind/body disconnect among
> African American women. (pp. 50-51)

In the spider's web, graft and craft meet. After all, these creatures "view the world suspended in the liminal space between heaven and earth" (Greene Benjamin, 2005, p. 54). The web spun by Jamaica Sweet in *See Now Then* is also the crossroads at which Aunt Nancy tends to Medusa.

Resisting Disease

The angry Mr. Sweet often imagines his spouse's severed head sitting on the yellow kitchen counter, her body scattered to the four corners of the earth (Kincaid, 2013, pp. 9-10; pp. 13-14; p. 85):

> But what if a surprise awaited for him just inside the
> door, for even a poor unfortunate man as he, for so Mr.
> Sweet thought of himself, unfortunate to be married
> to that bitch of woman born of beast; the surprise
> being the head of his wife just lying on the counter, her
> body never to be found, but her head severed from it,
> evidence that she could no longer block his progress in
> the world … (pp. 9-10)

Yet Mrs. Sweet persists in singing off-key, her head fixed upon her shoulders, and rather than send readers into sobs, the narrative as parody often sends us into fits of laughter. The many mythical embodiments of Mrs. Sweet as a weaver who is to be understood in relationship to stories of multiple cultural origins, speak to Carole Boyce Davies' (1994) affirmation that "multiply articulated" discourses of identity can be understood as working simultaneously, as being braided or woven together (p. 56). They may also lift an ancient curtain to reveal a Medusa laughing (see Cixous, 1976) at anger, a woman writing whose ever-changing body might just be stock for a g/crafted text: "… her torso like a very old tree—a silver maple—whose curiously twin trunks were all that remained after a violent storm that cut a broad swathe through a hillside, a dale, a meadow and such …" (Kincaid, 2013, p. 86). And so, Kincaid's literary grafting and crafting emerge finally as a resistance to disease, the disease of monoculture or deathly unicity.

In repairing damage and resisting disease, Kincaid's novel reveals itself to be as much about roots as it is about shoots. Just as the intertextual and intergeneric grafts discussed earlier reach up and out in new directions, the work's multiple roots burrow deep and wide. R. J. Garner (2013) notes that natural root grafting can enable trees that have sustained damage to survive by drawing on resources from the shared roots of distant neighbors (p. 35). The first definition provided by the *Oxford English Dictionary* of "radical" reads "of, belonging to a root or roots; fundamental or inherent in the natural processes of life, vital" ("Radical", 2017, A.1.a.). In *See Now Then*, we might, therefore, call the root grafting and crafting that feeds the novel through Ananse/ Aunt Nancy and Lilith, Medusa and Brer Rabbit a manifestation of life-sustaining radical difference.

Focused with Precision

To conclude, I would like to come back to the question of survival, and more specifically to what writing to save one's life has to do with anger. Speaking about the novel in her interview with *Guernica*, the author commented, "[T]he important thing isn't whether I'm angry. The more important thing is, is it true?" (Alleyne, 2013, para. 36). And here is an old, or rather an ancient question: where or what is the line between fiction and truth? What does that line tell us about the people we are, the people we can or cannot become, the good or the evil we are capable of and the meaning of being human? Can we lead good and truthful lives?

Kincaid's novel raises these questions about truth and about anger, and in so doing, *See Now Then* formulates a literary response to a question of capital importance, one rephrased by Judith Butler in her 2012 Adorno Prize lecture as, "Can one lead a good life in a bad life?" Butler reaffirms, following on Theodor Adorno and Hannah Arendt, that to live a good life means more than just surviving because "… life, as much as it requires survival, must be more than survival in order to be livable. … So, an overarching demand must be precisely for a livable life — that is a life that can be lived" (p. 15). A bad life, on the other hand, is a life rendered unlivable, to any varying extent, by the unequal distribution of precarity, inequality and forms of effacement. Though each of us leads an individual life, our lives are socially interdependent. As such, we collectively uphold the powers of inequality, are subject to the bad life and are vulnerable to effacement, to becoming ungrievable (i.e., "not worth supporting and protecting as a life by dominant schemes of value", Butler, 2012, p. 10). And so, to live a good life, we must actively embody practices of critique; "… there must be resistance to the bad life in order to pursue the good life." Resistance to the bad life, she explains, like birth, may involve suffering, but that suffering can "bring about a new way of life, a more livable life that opposes the differential distribution of precarity" (Butler, 2012, p. 18).

I would like to suggest that *See Now Then* is a literary practice of critique and, therefore, of resistance to the bad life. In the essay "The Uses of Anger: Women Responding to Racism," Audre Lorde (2007) writes, "Every woman has a well-stocked arsenal of anger potentially useful against those oppressions, personal and institutional, which brought that anger into being. Focused with precision it can become a powerful source of energy serving progress and change" (p. 127). Kincaid has focused anger with precision, using the aesthetic and ethical practice of literary grafting as a means to resist forms of effacement. Boldly pruning back the branches of the canon, she successfully undermines conventional literary hierarchies. Her grafts bring women's crafts to the fore and show how they tell us truths, turning anger into love through parody and laughter and reminding us, borrowing again from Lorde

(2007), that *"Everything can be used / except what is wasteful / (you will need / to remember this when you are accused of destruction)"* (p. 127).

> As the novel draws to a close, Mrs. Sweet contemplates her life:
> Oh Now, oh now, said Mrs. Sweet to herself, for she was then looking into an abyss, but that would be literature; for she was now looking into the shallow depths, a structural depression, but that would be geology; and at the bottom of this metaphor or just a true representation lay her life, the remains of it, the facts of it, the substance of it, the summation of it, the finality of it, the good-bye for now and see you later maybe of it, she had loved her life so much; and this was a surprise to her, that she had loved her life so much. (Kincaid, 2013, p. 173)

Her thoughts ring like an echo to Judith Butler: "It may be that the question of how to live a good life depends upon the power to lead a life as well as the sense of having a life, living a life or, indeed, the sense of being alive." In *See Now Then,* Mrs. Sweet is poised in just such a position as to take some measure of a life lived and of a life loved.

Kincaid's literary answer to Butler necessarily questions the line between fiction and truth, reminding us that certain truths are sweetest when told by fiction. In as much as the novel creates confusion between Mrs. Sweet and the author herself, it reminds us that as writers and as readers, we take subjective sustenance from the fruits of literature. The author encourages us to sympathize with the devil. For if Eden is long gone, and paradise lost, we still have resistance, we still can love life and, as long as we resist by tending to what sustains us, like at the end of the novel, spring will come again, with new fruits to survive and thrive upon.

References

Alleyne, L. K. (2013). Jamaica Kincaid: Does Truth Have a Tone? *Guernica: A Magazine of Global Arts and Politics.* Retrieved from https://www.guernicamag.com/does-truth-have-a-tone/

Atonal. *The Oxford Dictionary of Music,* 2nd ed. rev. *Oxford Music Online.* Oxford University Press. Retrieved from http://www.oxfordmusiconline.com.library3.webster.edu/subscriber/article/opr/t237/e617

Boyce Davies, C. (1994). *Black Women, Writing and Identity: Migrations of the Subject.* New York, NY: Taylor & Francis.

Bouson Brooks, J. (2005). *Jamaica Kincaid: Writing Memory, Writing Back to the Mother.* Albany, NY: State of New York University Press.

Bhabha, H. (2014). *The Location of Culture.* New York, NY: Routledge. (First published 1994).

Butler, J. (2012). Can one lead a good life in a bad one? *Radical Philosophy, 176,* 9-18.

Cixous, H. (1976). The Laugh of the Medusa. (K. Cohen and P. Cohen, Transl.). *Signs, 1*(4), 875-893. (First published 1975).

Donnell, A. (2005). *Twentieth Century Caribbean Literature: Critical Moments in Anglophone Literary History.* London: Routledge.

Garner, R. J. (2013) *The Grafter's Handbook.* 6th ed. White River Junction, VT: Chelsea Green Publishing. (First published 1947).

Genette, G. (1997). *Palimpsests: Literature in the Second Degree.* (C. Newman & C. Doubinsky, Trans.). Lincoln, NE: University of Nebraska Press. (Original work published 1982).

Gilroy, P. (1993). *The Black Atlantic: Modernity and Double Consciousness.* Cambridge, MA: Harvard University Press.

Greene Benjamin, S. (2005). Weaving the Web of Reintegration: Locating Aunt Nancy in *Praisesong for the Widow. MELUS, 30*(1), 49-67. Retrieved from http://www.jstor.org/stable/30029611

Griffiths, P. (2017). Serialism. *Grove Music Online. Oxford Music Online.* Oxford UP. Retrieved from http://www.oxfordmusiconline.com.library3.webster.edu/subscriber/article/grove/music/25459.

Grafting, n. *OED Online.* Oxford: Oxford UP. Accessed 19 May 2017.

Harris Chandler, J. (1983). *The Complete Tales of Uncle Remus.* R. Chase (Ed.). Boston, MA: Houghton Mifflin Company. (First published 1855).

Kincaid, J. (1989). *A Small Place.* New York, NY: Plume. (First published 1981).

Kincaid, J. (1992). Autobiography of a Dress. Retrieved from http://www.shortstoryproject.com/biography-of-a-dress/

Kincaid, J. (1997). *My Brother.* New York, NY: Farrar, Straus and Giroux.

Kincaid, J. (1999). *My Garden (Book):*. New York, NY: Farrar, Straus and Giroux.

Kincaid, J. (2002). *Lucy.* New York, NY: Farrar, Straus and Giroux. (First published 1990).

Kincaid, J. (2002). *Mr. Potter.* New York, NY: Farrar, Straus and Giroux.

Kincaid, J. (2005). *Among Flowers: A Walk in the Himalaya.* Washington, D.C.: National Geographic.

Kincaid, J. (2011). The Dean and Mrs. Hess. *Little Star, 2,* 54-74.

Kincaid, J. (2013). *See Now Then.* New York, NY: Farrar, Straus and Giroux.

Lam, F. (2015). Edna Lewis and the Black Roots of American Cooking. *The New York Times,* 8 October 2015. Retrieved from https://www.nytimes.com/2015/11/01/magazine/edna-lewis-and-the-black-roots-of-american-cooking.html

Loh, A. (2017). A Conversation with Jamaica Kincaid. *The American Reader.* Retrieved from http://theamericanreader.com/a-conversation-with-jamaica-kincaid/.

Lorde, A. (2007). *Sister Outsider.* Berkley, CA: Crossing Press. (First published 1984).

Lorde, A. (1982). *Zami: A New Spelling of My Name.* Freedom, CA: The Crossing Press.

Marshall, P. (1983). *Praisesong for the Widow.* New York, NY: Plume.

Mayorga, L. (2014). Aran Sweater. In A. Lynch and M. D. Strauss (Eds.). *Ethnic Dress in the United States: A Cultural Encyclopedia* (pp. 15-16). Lanham, MD: Rowman and Littlefield Publishers, Inc., pp. 15-16.

Mazoyer, M. & and Roudart, L. (2006). *A History of World Agriculture: From the Neolithic Age to Current Crisis.* (J. H. Membrez, trans.). New York, NY: Monthly Review Press.

O'Neill, M. (1992). Nika Hazelton, Whose Cookbooks Influenced U.S. Tastes, Dies at 84. *The New York Times,* 17 April. Rerieved from http://www.nytimes.com/1992/04/17/us/nika-hazelton-whose-cookbooks-influenced-us-tastes-dies-at-84.html

Radical, adj. and n. *OED Online.* Oxford UP, Accessed 07 July 2017.

Sendak, M. (1991). *Where the Wild Things Are.* New York, NY: Harper Collins. (First published 1963).

Sipress, D. (2013). Marcella Hazan Changed My Life. *The New Yorker.* Retrieved from http://www.newyorker.com/culture/culture-desk/marcella-hazan-changed-my-life

Walker, S. (2001). Everyday Africa in New Jersey: Wonderings and Wanderings in the African Diaspora. In S. S. Walker (Ed.). *African Roots/American Cultures: Africa in the Creation of the Americas* (pp. 45-80). Lanham, MD: Rowman and Littlefield Publishers, Inc.

Wise Brown, M. (1991). *Goodnight Moon.*1947. New York, NY: Harper. (First published 1947).

Wise Brown, M. (1972). *The Runaway Bunny.* New York, NY: Harper. (First published 1942).

Woolf, V. (1989). *A Room of One's Own.* Ontario, FL: Harcourt Brace Jovanovich. (First published 1929).

FOUR

JAMAICA KINCAID AND OLIVE SENIOR GARDENING THROUGH HISTORY, CULTIVATING RHIZOMIC SUBJECTIVITIES

Myriam Moïse
CNRS, Université des Antilles, LC2S

Contact : Myriam Moïse, CNRS, Université des Antilles, LC2S
myriam.moise@univ-antilles.fr
To cite this article:
[Myriam Moïse. "Jamaica Kincaid and Olive Senior Gardening through History, Cultivating Rhizomic Subjectivities." *Wagadu: A Journal of Transnational Women's and Gender Studies,* Summer 2018, vol. 19, pp. 43-53]

Abstract

This analysis of texts by Jamaica Kincaid and Olive Senior focuses on their representations of landscapes and their re-envisioning of the scarred lands historically cultivated by their African enslaved ancestors.

Gardening through history is a process of feminine resistance, a genuine metaphor for plowing into one's land and repossessing one's body.

Ancestor on the auction block

> Across the years
> I look
> I see you sweating, toiling, suffering
> Within your loins I see the seed
> Of multitudes
> From your labour
> Grow roads, aqueducts, cultivation
> A new country is born
> Yours was the task to clear the ground
> Mine be the task to build (Vera Bell, 1948).

Jamaican poet Vera Bell draws a link between the scarred lands historically cultivated by her enslaved ancestors and the writer's task to re-explore this land in order to rebuild and create new spaces. Part of the African diasporic woman writer's task thus consists in re-exploring and re-envisioning the land in order to achieve self-recreation. The imagery of gardening through history is used as a process of feminine resistance and a genuine metaphor for plowing the earth, repossessing one's land and reclaiming one's right to self-definition. Traditionally, the land is linked to femininity and in this respect, Ben Heller's questions in "Landscape, Femininity and Caribbean Discourse" are highly significant: "How does one write from the Caribbean as a woman, when Caribbean landscape and culture are themselves metaphorized as feminine? Will a woman writer be better able to 'savor the meaning' of her land because, on a metaphorical level at least, she is that land?" (p. 3). What this paper proposes to demonstrate is that Kincaid and Senior develop an umbilical relationship with their land, which is omnipresent in their work, and how the reconstruction of their diasporic female subjectivities may depend on gardening and digging into this land. The following analysis is centred on Jamaica Kincaid's non-fiction book *My*

Garden (Book): and Olive Senior's poetry book *Gardening in the Tropics*, so as to explore the two authors' representations of the garden and their experience of Edouard Glissant's model of "complicity of relation" to the land (1997, p. 147), "a model that is flexible enough to bring together places linked by history and geography" (DeLoughrey, p. xi).

Beyond its universality and the numerous thematic perspectives it offers, the garden imagery appears to encompass a deeper meaning in the works of Kincaid and Senior. The archetypal garden is undoubtedly the Garden of Eden, but mythical gardens include the Garden of Eros and Psyche and the Garden of the Hesperides in Greek mythology, or the biblical Gethsemane Garden, among many others. The garden offers several levels of interpretation: it is considered on the one hand as a cultural, spiritual and peaceful space where humans can achieve harmony and self-fulfilment, but it is also a space of temptation, boredom, and rebellion, and a place where good and evil, feminine and masculine, nature and culture interact and overlap. The garden is also linked to a sexual dimension; for instance, Haitian writer René Depestre celebrates the garden-woman in his *Alleluia pour une femme-jardin*, thus intrinsically linking the garden to the feminine space. This connection between woman and garden is reminiscent of the numerous representations of human beings transformed into plants in classical mythology; the garden can become a space of recreation, transmutation and cross-pollination. The idea of cross-pollination is essential, as the pollen is transferred from one flower to another, just as cultures meet to create new cultures. It is this process of cross-fertilization in space that Kincaid and Senior appear to associate with the production of discourse.

Gardening through history is a genuine process of cultural transplantation, one that is reminiscent of Deleuze and Guattari's theory of the "rhizome" (1980) and Glissant's creolisation (1990), in which the root is not conceived in terms of singularity anymore, but in terms of plurality and multirootedness. Deleuze and Guattari describe the rhizome as an "antigenealogy," and as an alternative to the single root that implied fixity and 'pure' origins. The rhizome is indeed "a means of propagation which operates underground, without hierarchies, connecting multiple points, places and identities" (p. 21). Through Edouard Glissant's poetics of 'Creolisation,' Caribbean identities themselves are specifically depicted as fluid and multi-rooted; "the concept of the rhizome maintains the idea of rootedness but challenges that of a totalitarian root" (1997, p. 11). For their rhizomic identities to flourish, Olive Senior and Jamaica Kincaid need to relocate the site of the historical and transform gardening into an intimate activity through which digging into the earth becomes a way of investigating one's past and redefining oneself. Senior's poem "The Knot Garden" foresees environmental fertilization within a mixture of various species: "Gardening in the Tropics, / you'll find things that don't / belong together often intertwine / all mixed up in this amazing fecundity" (Senior, 1994, p. 88). Kincaid particularly embraces the concept of the rhizome when she describes the gardener figure as an unstable being: "that gardener, any gardener, is not a stable being; that gardener, any gardener, is not a model of consistency" (Kincaid, 2001, p. 224).

To Jamaica Kincaid, the garden is the wider garden of the earth; her conception of a borderless and fluid garden space innovatively turns into a space of memory. At the beginning of *My Garden (Book):*, when the female narrator does not manage to grow flowers from seeds because of an unprepared soil, she underlines the necessity to plow the land, and sees gardening as "an exercise in memory, a way of getting to a past that is [her] own" (Kincaid, 2001, p. 8). Kincaid's unexpected garden metaphors have not always been sufficiently taken at face value by critics.

> In the penultimate section entitled "The garden I have in mind," the narrator states:
> I first came to the garden with practicality in mind, a real beginning that would lead to a real end: where to get this, how to grow that … but in the end, I came to know how to grow the things I like to grow, looking – at other people's gardens. I imagine they acquired knowledge

of such things in much the same way – looking and
looking at somebody else's garden.

But we who covet our neighbor's garden must finally
return to our own, with all its ups and downs, its
disappointments, its rewards. (pp. 219-220)

This passage illustrates Kincaid's need to develop a representation of a
garden beyond normative limits, hence beyond linear definitions. Seeing
space and representing one's own space participate in constructing one's
identity beyond borders. Looking at one's neighbour's garden is depicted
as a necessary initial activity in order to transcend one's individual
borders, but one cannot content oneself with imitation, as one must
always return to one's own original garden space. The gardener is
therefore depicted as an individual in need of self-construction and self-
discovery within the very space of the garden. While the importance of
history is underlined throughout the text, disappointments and rewards,
ups and downs, must still be embraced in order to grasp a genuine sense
of the very garden; it is a liminal garden which is described by Kincaid,
one which allows individuals to teeter between spaces and recreate
themselves while gardening through history. In this sense, compared
to the environment depicted in Kincaid's well-known essay *A Small
Place*, the space of the garden in *My Garden (Book):* appears much
broader and expandable. The garden that the narrator has in mind is
an imaginary garden, a limitless space which is not static. In fact, the
narrator questions the gardeners' wish to remain within "the borders
they cultivate, the space in the garden they occupy" (p. 217). This phrase
works as a leitmotiv in the text; the narrator repeats it so as to emphasize
the necessity to transcend borders and shun limited spaces. The garden is
described as a limitless geocultural place, and a space of memory which
influences identity construction: "Memory is a gardener's real palette;
memory as it summons up the past, memory as it shapes the present,
memory as it dictates the future" (pp. 218-19). Kincaid's garden is at
the crossroads of time and histories; in her garden essay, the narrator's
personal history mingles with collective History. The recurrent allusions

or comparisons inserted between brackets throughout the essay allow the reader to get an insight into the configurations between the space of the garden and the female emotional space, whether it is frustration, envy or something else.

In *My Garden Book:*, the imagery of the plant embodies the complex identity construction for African diasporic women, and the mother figure, a noted Kincaidian obsession, has a strong, if subtle, presence throughout:

> We come to it with a blindness, plus a jumble of feelings
> that mere language (as far as I can see) seems inadequate
> to express, to define an attachment that is so ordinary:
> a plant loved especially for something endemic to it: (it
> cannot help its situation: it loves the wet, it loves the dry,
> it reminds the person seeing it of a wave or a waterfall
> or some event that contains so personal an experience as
> when my mother would not allow me to do something
> I particularly wanted to do and in my misery I noticed
> that the frangipani tree was in bloom). (p. 220)

In this passage the blooming vegetation comes in contrast with a restricted female nature and a disciplined female body through the constant motherly presence, even though it appears between brackets, in ways reminiscent of Kincaid's short story "Girl" in *At the Bottom of the River*. The sacred and healing symbolism of the blooming frangipani tree cannot be fully perceived by the narrator, whose senses appear to be restrained by the spiritual presence of her mother. Contrasting with the female body, plants are allowed to exist in contradiction, having their needs and desires respected, whether it is through fluidity or drought; they bloom beyond restriction. However, sound and vision appear as altered, and the narrator concludes that language cannot capture the emotion inspired by the garden, as though imagining new textual and cultural geographies would require a special language. As Gwendolyn Henderson puts it in her 1989 essay "Speaking in

Tongues: Dialogics, Dialectics, and the Black Woman Writer's Literary Tradition," diasporic women writers may well have to develop a specific tongue which "transforms soundlessness into utterance, unity into diversity, formlessness into form, chaos into art, silence into tongues, glossolalia into heteroglossia" (p. 36). Jamaica Kincaid truly entices the reader to a discursive voyage through her own garden but it remains an unsatisfactory garden, as she concludes that "a garden, no matter how good it is, must never completely satisfy. The world as we know it, after all, began in a very good garden, a completely satisfying garden – Paradise – but after a while the owner and the occupants wanted more" (Kincaid, 2001, p. 220).

Kincaid's denunciation of the shortcomings of human beings finds strong echoes in Senior's iconic poem "Meditation on Yellow," in which the poetic voice cannot bear the greed of colonizers and eventually gives up the land and entire nature: "I give you the gold/ I give you the land/ I give you the breeze/ I give you the beaches/ I give you the yellow sand… I can't give anymore" (Senior, 1994, p. 15-16). While Senior's poetic voice is highly critical of the hegemonic figure of the colonizer as dispossessing Jamaican natives and original gardeners, Kincaid's *My Garden Book:* depicts a gardener who embraces multiple identities. In her section entitled "The Garden in Eden" (Kincaid, 2001, p. 221), the gardener is a female God-like figure imposing the specific "layout" of a garden which is not satisfactory to its occupants, Adam and Eve. Kincaid uses the original garden to illustrate the necessity to position oneself in space and further rejects stable spaces. Both gardener and occupants are therefore described as unstable human beings as "any gardener is not a model of consistency" (p. 224). To Kincaid, it seems that claiming the right to garden one's own space and cultivate one's own patch of land is a metaphor for cultivating one's own identity beyond limited spaces, beyond normative gardens. Above all, it is the right for complex and unexpected beings and spaces to exist which is claimed: "Eden is like that, so rich in comfort, it tempts me to cause discomfort; I am in a state of constant discomfort and I like this state so much I would like to share it" (p. 229). This final statement further highlights Kincaid's refusal of stable and comfortable spaces, perhaps because the diasporic female experience of space is one of instability and discomfort, one that she wishes to share with others through discourse. This very discomfort is also historical as it is linked to the original displacement of black women expelled from their African garden.

Kincaid's 'discomfort' finds strong resonances in Senior's poetry, in which gardening is not pictured as a peaceful activity; one never knows what can be found when digging into the earth. In fact, at the beginning of her poetry collection *Gardening in the Tropics,* Senior's poetic voice warns us about the remains of the past that may be found while gardening in the tropics: "Gardening in the Tropics, you never know what you'll turn up. Quite often, bones" (p. 85). Senior's poetic language is reminiscent of Edouard Glissant's "language of landscape" (1989, p. 145), as the Caribbean flora is constantly personified through the device known as pathetic fallacy. A mixture of Jamaican Patois and Standard English, Senior's *Gardening in the Tropics* epitomizes the author's hybrid language and counter-exotic meditation on landscape. In these collections, the Caribbean flora is personified through her multiple pigments, her capacity to resist, to reproduce and cross-fertilize under all circumstances. Just as in Kincaid's *My Garden Book:*, Senior's re-envisioning of the land is not static, as her symbolism is often ambivalent. In the poem "Plants," the poetic voice portrays plants as "deceptive" and personifies them as invaders and conquerors of space. The five opening stanzas provide an ample description of the plants which reads as an allegory of colonialism through adjectives such as "exhibitionist," "prolific," "imperialistic," "invasive," "explosive," or through the use of present participles like "clinging," "anchoring," or "colonizing" (p. 63). However, Senior does not limit herself to the classic colonial imagery, but rather invites her reader to go beyond apparent meaning and consider a different form of colonisation, one that no human being can control:

> Maybe you haven't quite taken in the
> colonizing ambitions of hitchhiking

> burrs on your sweater, surf-riding nuts
> bobbing on ocean, parachuting seeds and other
>
> airborne traffic dropping in … (p. 63)

The above stanza suddenly opens a different perspective as it suggests the unavoidable fecundity of plants through the motif of the seed ('burrs,' 'nuts,' 'seeds'), as well as through the semantic field of motion and displacement, which is omnipresent in the poem: 'running around,' 'dispersal,' 'hitchhiking,' 'surf-riding,' 'parachuting,' 'dropping in' (p. 63). The choice of verbs further denotes the author's wish to cover every possible type of transportation including land, air or water transport, as if to force the reader to consider the global nature of the seed. The seed then becomes a natural coloniser that no one can prevent from reproducing itself in any time and space, and in this respect, perhaps Senior's poetic vision of the seed may appear to embrace her representation of the native people of Jamaica, the Taìnos. Despite historical extermination and brutal colonisation, the Taìno people and, by extension local Jamaicans, are subtly allegorised as constantly moving, thus reproducing and flowering. The many occurrences of the word "seed" in the poem come to underline the importance of the process of reproduction, regeneration and cross-pollination.

> … And what
> about those special agents called flowers?
> Dressed, perfumed, and made-up for romancing
> insects, bats, birds, bees, even you –
>
> don't deny it, my dear, I've seen you
>
> sniff and exclaim. Believe me, Innocent,
> that sweet fruit, that berry is nothing
> more than ovary, the instrument to seduce
> you into scattering plant progeny. Part of
> a vast cosmic program that once set

in motion cannot be undone though we
become plant food and earth wind down.
They'll outlast us, they were always there … (pp. 63-64)

The assonances in [i] reinforce the link between the 'berry' fruit and the 'ovary,' the female reproductive organ; 'berry' and 'ovary' not only rhyme, but also establish a link with the planted grain, and notions of fecundity, fertility and maternity. The berry imagery also has historical resonances with Christopher Columbus's first exchange with the Taìnos and the Shakespearian scene between Prospero and Caliban where the first offers the latter "water with berries" in order to get his help. Barbadian author George Lamming's novel *Water with Berries* (1971) rewrites the colonial encounter and refers to this scene in Shakespeare's *The Tempest*, where Caliban rebels against Prospero.[viii] The word 'berry' designates a fleshy fruit producing many seeds and as a suffix, it has given birth to a variety of names of fruit. Senior's focus on the berry certainly denotes her wish to enhance the power of hybridization of the berry/ovary and the cultural process of multiplying and grafting objects/subjects onto the same root. In the last line quoted above ('They'll outlast us, they were always there'), the reader is reminded of the eternal nature of plants and vegetation, which will always precede humanity and resist through the power of their seeds, hence through the continuous pollination process.

The significance of the seed is surely an omnipresent motif in Kincaid's *My Garden Book:*, from the very start when she mentions that her husband's gift for Mother's Day included some flower seeds that she immediately planted in a patch of land that had never been cultivated, but "nothing grew, the ground was improperly prepared, it was in the shade of a big oak tree and a big maple tree" (Kincaid, 2001, p. 4). The oak tree and the maple tree seem to be personified as vegetal hegemonies in Kincaid's text, these two trees whose resistance has prevented her first seeds from growing. In Senior's poetry, the embodiment of resistance is found within Jamaican biodiversity as the immutability of a number of natural elements of the Caribbean flora is emphasised. For instance, the bamboo becomes a symbol for resistance and immortality, perhaps a reference to history, memory and generational transfer. As for the pineapple and the papaya, they both represent potential dangers. Apparently welcoming, juicy and sweet, the eyes of the pineapple are actually spying; this is perhaps another reference to traditional Caribbean societies, where young women are constantly watched and expected to behave in certain ways, echoing Kincaid's authoritarian mother figure. In the diasporic context, the pineapple may also be the allegory of North American societies where Kincaid and Senior have relocated, both welcoming and threatening, both regenerative and oppressive.

Contrasting with the resistant natural elements, Senior's poem "Discovery" depicts a fragile landscape through the imagery of the mangrove swamp, which constitutes a fertile tropical habitat sheltering a number of species in its breast:

> Always
> Like the futile march of crab-armies
> From mangrove fortress to the beach
>
> Always
> Like the palm-fringe waiting
> to be breached
>
> Already I know, the moment you land
> I become islanded
>
> In the shadows of the rain forest
> I wait in submission
>
> Amidst the trembling of the leaves
> I practice hesitant discourse
>
> Always
> my impenetrable heart. (Senior, 2005, p. 44)

The homophony of the words 'breach' and 'beach' reflects the fragility and fragmentation of a feminized landscape and the sea. Caribbean space is depicted as fragile in Senior's poetry in which the land is fragmented and is still being deflowered by neo-colonisation. The rape of the land is compared to the deflowering of the female body, thus resonating with an ecofeminist poetics. Often revealing a certain feminisation of the land, Senior's poetry exploits the 'I/(s)land' imagery to link the shaping of Caribbean landscapes to the construction of the physical and discursive body/self. The female characters that Senior depicts in her poetry as well as in her prose often blend into the Caribbean landscapes and despite the hardships of life, they demonstrate great capacities for resistance and self-recreation. Senior's "Discovery" betrays normative expectations as it announces the degradation of the land through processes of colonisation and tourist activities. Mocking the tourist who comes to visit the island, the poet ironically points out the fleeting effects produced by Jamaican landscapes. She overtly criticises tourism as a neo-colonial enterprise through the poetic voice's ironically inviting the tourist to enjoy for the very last time the beauty and virginity of rivers, mountains and seas, before they are invaded and degraded by the excesses of modern progress. To Senior, identities appear to grow as plants, that is to say that even though they are damaged, the roots remain and can be grafted, replanted, and fertilized into a transcultural being; this suggests the immortality of African Caribbean memories and identities. Through Senior's verses, the planted seed becomes the symbol of spatial invasion and of transplantation, and its hybrid crop comes to feed the memory of the Caribbean people and contribute to the pollination of the text. Senior's landscapes are at times connected and at others detached, they symbolise the diasporic identities that transcend national barriers and promote a transnational conception of spaces made of fragments of cultures and discontinued histories. As Stuart Hall explains, "identity is formed at the unstable point where the 'unspeakable' stories of subjectivity meet the narratives of history, of a culture" (1996, p. 115).

Gardening through history occurs within a non-linear time, which allows the Caribbean subject to start anew and transcend space and time, as St Lucian poet and Nobel laureate Derek Walcott puts it: "The Caribbean sensibility is not marinated in the past. It is not exhausted. It is new. But it is its complexity, not its historically explained simplicities, which is new" (p. 124). Kincaid's work is an embodiment of this constant renewal, as she explores these historical complexities, remaps new spaces that are expandable and non-linear. To Jamaica Kincaid, the garden is a fluid space which is "so bound up with words about the garden, with words themselves, that any set idea of the garden, any set picture, is a provocation to [her]" (Kincaid, 2001, p. 7). As a matter of fact, both Senior and Kincaid see the garden space as one that allows fluidity and transcends preconceived definitions of the self. To these two diasporic Caribbean writers, recreating and reimagining the land entails the creation of specific discursive and poetic environments where natural and transcultural elements are in constant dialogue and in communion with the diasporic mind. Kincaid and Senior use the garden imagery to enhance the existence of boundless cultures and alternative conceptions of history, space and identity. Through their specific representations of the garden, Kincaid and Senior express their need to cultivate new female identities and allow the growth and fertilization of new cultures. In Stuart Hall's words, "diaspora identities are those which are constantly producing and reproducing themselves anew, through transformation and difference" (Hall and du Gay, 1996b, p. 436), and the two authors' discursive gardening through history emphasizes their interest in the mystery of identity construction, in defining who they are. Their writings foreground the very complexity of diasporic female subjectivities that are situated at the very heart of their transcultural and borderless gardens.

References

Bell, V. (2005). Ancestor on the Auction Block. In S. Brown and M. McWatt (Eds.). *The Oxford Book of Caribbean Verse* (pp. 28-29). (First published 1948).

Deleuze, G. and F. Guattari. (2004). *A Thousand Plateaus: Capitalism and Schizophrenia.* Volume 2. (B. Massumi, Trans.). London and New York, NY: Continuum. (Original work published 1980)

DeLoughrey, E. M. (2007). *Routes and Roots: Navigating Caribbean and Pacific Island Literatures.* Honolulu, HI: University of Hawaii Press.

Depestre, R. (1973). *Alleluia pour une femme-jardin: récits d'amour solaire.* Montréal: Éditions Leméac.

Glissant, E. (1989). *Caribbean Discourse: Selected Essays.* (J. M. Dash, Trans.). Charlottesville, VA: University Press of Virginia. (Original work published 1981).

______. (1997). *Poetics of Relation.* (B. Wing, Trans.). Ann Arbor, MI: University of Michigan Press. (Original work published 1990).

Hall, S. (1996a). Minimal Selves. In A. H. Baker, M. Diawara & R. H. Lindeborg (Eds.). *Black British Cultural Studies* (pp. 114-119). Chicago, IL: University of Chicago Press.

Hall, S. and P. du Gay (Eds.). (1996b). *Questions of Cultural Identity.* London: Sage Publications.

Heller, B. (1996. Landscape, Femininity and Caribbean Discourse. *Modern Language Notes 111*(2), 391-416.

Henderson, G. M. (1994). Speaking in Tongues: Dialogics, Dialectics and the Black Woman Writer's Literary Tradition. In P. Williams and L. Chrisman (Eds.). *Colonial Discourse and Post-Colonial Theory: A Reader* (pp. 257-267). New York, NY: Columbia University Press.

Kincaid, J. (1988). *A Small Place.* New York, NY: Farrar, Straus and Giroux.

Kincaid, J. (1983). Girl. *At the Bottom of the River.* New York, NY: Farrar, Straus and Giroux. (First published 1978).

Kincaid, J. *My Garden (Book):.* (2001). New York, NY: Farrar, Straus and Giroux. (First published 1999).

Lamming, G. (1971). *Water with Berries.* Kingston: Longman Caribbean.

Senior, O. (1994). *Gardening in the Tropics.* Toronto: Insomniac Press.

Senior, O. (2005). Discovery. *Over the Roofs of the World.* Toronto: Insomniac Press.

Shakespeare, W. (1863). *The Tempest.* London: Macmillan and Co.

Walcott, D. (1970). What the Twilight Says: An Overture. *Dream on Monkey Mountain and Other Plays* (pp. 3-40). New York, NY: Farrar, Straus and Giroux.

FIVE

GREFFE, BOUTURE ET CRÉOLISATION: JARDINS DE MOTS ET DE SENS CHEZ KINCAID

Pauline Amy de La Bretèque
Sorbonne Université

Contact : Pauline Amy de La Bretèque, Sorbonne Université
pauline.amydelabreteque@gmail.com
To cite this article:
[Pauline Amy de La Bretèque. « Greffe, bouture et creolisation : Jardins de mots et de sens chez Kincaid. » *Wagadu: A Journal of Transnational Women's and Gender Studies*, Summer 2018, vol. 19, pp. 54-65]

Abstract

Kincaid aborde la botanique comme cadre de réflexion sur la colonisation, l'identité et la créolisation. Comment la créolisation est-elle exprimée à travers la métaphore botanique ? La greffe et la bouture participent d'une « éco-poétique » de la créolisation : les mots se greffent, produisant un texte qui se créolise.

Les écrits botaniques de Jamaica Kincaid remontent aux années 1990, années durant lesquelles elle a publié une série d'articles dans *The New Yorker*. La publication de deux ouvrages, *My Garden (Book):* en 1999 et *Among Flowers* en 2005, s'inscrit dans la continuité des travaux parus dans ce magazine. Kincaid, originaire de l'île d'Antigua, vit à présent dans le Vermont où elle cultive son jardin, fait des commandes de plantes onéreuses aux pépinières et part en exploration dans l'Himalaya afin de récolter des graines. *My Garden (Book):* et *Among Flowers* dépeignent bien sûr ces activités mais vont au-delà d'un simple intérêt du jardinage pour le jardinage. Kincaid aborde la botanique et le jardinage comme cadres de réflexion métaphoriques sur la colonisation, l'identité et la créolisation.

Dans cet article, je m'intéresserai particulièrement à la poétique de créolisation dans *Among Flowers* et *My Garden (Book):*. La créolisation, telle qu'elle a été définie par Édouard Glissant, est « une rencontre d'éléments culturels venus d'horizons absolument divers et qui . . . s'imbriquent et se confondent l'un dans l'autre pour donner quelque chose d'absolument imprévisible, d'absolument nouveau et qui est la réalité créole » (Glissant, 1996, p. 15). Le concept de créolisation est un concept clef dans la représentation de la Caraïbe. La quasi-extermination des populations amérindiennes, l'installation de colons européens, l'importation d'esclaves d'Afrique de l'Ouest puis de travailleurs venus d'Asie en font un espace exceptionnellement divers et unique, puisqu'aucune population ne peut se proclamer originaire de cette région.

Le processus de créolisation rejoint le principe du procédé de greffe qui consiste à unir une partie d'une plante et une partie d'une autre dans le but de former une plante nouvelle. De plus, la question de la créolisation implique celle de l'exil qui est essentielle à la colonisation mais aussi à un monde globalisé. C'est là que l'image de la bouture, ce fragment végétal que l'on détache d'une plante et que l'on place dans un milieu où il prend racine et se développe en une plante complète, reflète le processus de créolisation. La problématique de l'adaptation et de l'acclimatation est centrale dans les écrits botaniques de Jamaica Kincaid, qu'il s'agisse de son voyage dans l'Himalaya ou de ses réflexions sur la notion de jardin botanique.

Dans un premier temps, j'analyserai le jardin comme espace de la créolisation et la manière dont les procédés de greffe et de bouture participent d'une créolisation botanique. Je montrerai aussi l'importance de cette créolisation botanique dans la redécouverte et la réappropriation de l'environnement, passage nécessaire de la quête identitaire et de la décolonisation de soi. Dans un deuxième temps, j'envisagerai la greffe et la bouture comme métaphores de l'entreprise coloniale et leur lien avec une créolisation culturelle. Là, je soulignerai la différence primordiale entre les métaphores de la greffe et de la bouture et les problèmes que celles-ci soulèvent. Je terminerai par une analyse de la greffe et de la bouture comme procédés linguistique et artistique participant d'une « écopoétique » (Savory, 2011) de la créolisation.

Greffe et bouture : une créolisation botanique

Le paysage de la Caraïbe a été profondément transformé par la colonisation. Les ressources de la nature caribéenne ont été exploitées quasiment jusqu'à épuisement et beaucoup d'espèces se sont éteintes au cours des deux derniers siècles. Selon Édouard Glissant (1981), le système des plantations a complètement aliéné l'homme de son environnement dans les Caraïbes. La nature a été réduite à sa fonction économique et le colonialisme a véritablement produit de nouveaux paysages (Mastnak, Elyachar et Boellstorff, 2014). De plus, la représentation des paysages caribéens n'a longtemps été faite que d'un point de vue européen. Kincaid dans *Lucy*, dénonce la vision de la nature imposée par l'éducation coloniale, notamment à travers le poème de Wordsworth « I Wandered Lonely as a Cloud » décrivant un parterre de jonquilles. Elle voue une haine aux jonquilles car ces fleurs lui ont été imposées comme symboles du printemps. Or, pour elle qui avait grandi dans les Caraïbes, les jonquilles, et même le printemps ne faisaient référence à rien de connu. Andrée-Anne Kekeh-Dika qualifie les jonquilles de Wordsworth chez Kincaid de « résidu marquant de l'imposition d'un savoir colonial aliénant » (Kekeh-Dika, p. 40). Maryse Condé insiste sur la nécessité de s'affranchir de l'identification à la nature européenne : « La connaissance du moi n'est pas possible sans l'appropriation de l'univers géographique qui le sous-tend. » (Condé, 1998, p. 2). C'est pourquoi Glissant souligne la nécessaire re-présentation et ré-imagination du paysage caribéen par les Caribéens eux-mêmes, notamment par la littérature. Ainsi, à travers ses écrits botaniques, Kincaid se réapproprie la nature, elle la représente à nouveau et, elle va plus loin que cela puisqu'elle reproduit dans *My Garden (Book):* la Caraïbe par la carte de l'archipel formée par les parterres de fleurs (pp. 7-8). Kincaid réinvente ses relations avec la nature, qui ne sont plus aliénées par l'intermédiaire colonial puisqu'elle entretient un lien physique avec les plantes qu'elle cultive : elle recrée cette nature de son propre point de vue.

La nature caribéenne comporte de nombreuses plantes importées durant la période coloniale. Des espèces végétales maintenant considérées comme emblématiques du paysage caribéen sont en fait venues d'ailleurs : l'arbre à pain par exemple, a été importé d'Océanie pour nourrir les esclaves, la canne à sucre, élément majeur du paysage caribéen, est originaire de Nouvelle-Guinée ou encore le café, venant d'Afrique et d'Asie. Les esclaves eux-mêmes ont apporté avec eux des graines lors de la traversée de l'Atlantique, ce qui explique à l'heure actuelle la présence d'ignames originaires d'Afrique dans la Caraïbe par exemple. De même, Jamaica Kincaid conçoit un jardin dans le Vermont à partir de plantes venues de divers horizons. Ainsi, par le jardinage, l'écrivaine recrée et réinvente la nature caribéenne dans sa diversité : des plantes venant de partout, rapportées de l'Himalaya même, qui se mêlent et s'imbriquent dans un même espace, celui du jardin. De plus, elle décrit au début de *My Garden (Book):* son jardin et les différentes espèces qui s'y entremêlent. Elle écrit à propos de la *Wisteria floribunda* (la glycine du Japon) :

> it throws out long, twining stems, mixing itself up with
> the canes of the *Rosa* 'Alchymist,' which is growing
> not too nearby, mixing itself up with a honeysuckle

(*Lonicera*) and even going far away to twine itself around
a red rose (*Rosa* 'Henry Kelsy'). (p. 11)

Ce passage évoque l'entrelacement des différentes plantes, qui viennent toutes de régions différentes du monde : la glycine floribonde vient du Japon (importée aux États-Unis dans les années 1830) et la rose, originaire de Chine, est l'une des espèces végétales qui a subi le plus de modifications et d'hybridations : la *Rosa* 'Henry Kelsey' et la *Rosa* 'Alchymist' sont toutes deux des roses hybrides modernes, issues de greffes. D'autres plantes greffées sont mentionnées, comme les *delphiniums* par exemple ou le *Lilium orientalis*. Ce jardin que Kincaid recréé dans le Vermont reflète la diversité de celui de ses parents à Antigua qui comportait un arbre à pain, des cannes à sucre, un corossol et un papayer originaires d'Amérique Centrale. Dans *Among Flowers,* elle mange au Népal des christophines, un légume qui pousse aussi dans les Antilles : le même légume peut être consommé d'un bout à l'autre de la planète (p. 43). Elle retrouve aussi dans un village de l'Himalaya des plantes du Mexique comme le bougainvillier (p. 65).

Il faut tout de même préciser que Kincaid elle-même ne pratique pas de greffe, procédé qui, contrairement à la bouture, est difficilement réalisable par les jardiniers amateurs, mais plutôt réalisé par les pépiniéristes auxquels Kincaid achète ses plantes. La greffe est une pratique complexe qui demande du matériel spécifique puisqu'elle consiste à implanter un bourgeon ou un fragment de plante dans les tissus d'une autre plante ou de la même plante. La bouture, au contraire, ne requiert aucun matériel, puisqu'il s'agit simplement de détacher un fragment d'une plante et de le laisser prendre racine et se développer en terre. Le jardin de Kincaid comporte une grande diversité de plantes mais une attention particulière est accordée aux plantes « indigènes » à son jardin, comme les roses de Mrs. Woodworth qu'elle tient absolument à conserver.

"The garden was to me more than the garden as I used to think of it » (p. 6). Ici, Kincaid affirme clairement que son jardin est plus qu'un jardin : elle injecte, ou plutôt elle greffe du sens au végétal. L'auteure et son mari achètent une maison ayant appartenu à Robert Woodworth, un ancien botaniste. Ses trois fils viennent récupérer dans la maison les choses qui leur tiennent à cœur : l'un d'entre eux prend des boutures des roses de sa mère, qui elle-même les avait prises dans le jardin de sa propre mère. La valeur affective et spirituelle des végétaux est ainsi mise en valeur. Un peu plus loin dans *My Garden (Book):*, un paysagiste conseille à Kincaid de couper les arbres dans son nouveau jardin puisqu'ils ne présentent aucun intérêt botanique. Après quoi Kincaid va s'excuser auprès des arbres : « I do not find such a gesture, apologizing to the trees, laughable. » (p. 34). Par le jardinage et les techniques d'hybridation que sont la greffe et la bouture, Kincaid renouvelle ses relations avec la nature. Elle représente aussi une nature créolisée, issue du mélange entre diverses espèces de plantes. La nature n'est pas réduite à sa fonction économique. Le jardin est ainsi perçu comme un espace de créolisation et d'hybridation où la nature à laquelle Kincaid greffe du sens, retrouve une valeur spirituelle.

Métaphore botanique de la colonisation
et de la créolisation

DeLoughrey, Handley et Gosson établissent un parallèle entre créolisation culturelle et créolisation botanique : « [there are i]nextricable links between the history of human and botanical transplantation, the region's cultural and social hybridity, and the fate of the landscape's biodiversity » (2005, p. 19). La Caraïbe est en effet un espace où les êtres humains (venus d'Europe, d'Afrique ou d'Asie), comme les plantes, ont été transplantés dans un nouvel environnement. Les plantes dans les œuvres botaniques de Kincaid semblent donc représenter la population des Caraïbes. Ainsi, différentes cultures venues avec ces populations, à l'image des plantes, ont été bouturées dans la Caraïbe, où elles s'adaptent à leur nouvel environnement.

À travers le jardin, Kincaid affirme le caractère hybride et créolisé de la nature caribéenne. Selon Jonathan Stouck (2005), revendiquer la créolisation de la nature, c'est revendiquer celle de ses habitants :

Like plants, people must have a firm ground or basis on which to develop their sense of self, yet must also seek new possibilities in rhizome-like migrations. The garden is a vital metaphor for contemporary identity negotiations not only in its history, which addresses issues of belonging and exclusion, but also in its potential for both propagation and differentiation. (p. 120)

Les jardins et les paysages sont le reflet de l'histoire (l'histoire coloniale et celle des plantations) mais sont aussi espaces d'échange et d'interaction. Alors, la bouture peut être perçue comme une métaphore de la migration et de l'exil, de la transplantation des êtres humains et du bouturage de leurs cultures. Une fois transplantées, ces différentes cultures se greffent les unes aux autres pour former quelque chose d'absolument nouveau qui est la réalité créole. Ces greffes, ces créolisations culturelles sont le résultat d'un processus forcé et violent qui est celui de la colonisation et de la déportation, de la violence originelle du passage du Milieu, décrit par Édouard Glissant comme un « gouffre-matrice » et de « l'arrachement » (Glissant, 1990, p. 17) au pays d'origine. Les plantes du jardin de Kincaid, leurs mélanges et leur diversité seraient donc autant d'images de la culture caribéenne, issue du déracinement, de la bouture puis de la greffe de différentes cultures venues d'horizons différents. Ainsi, toutes ces plantes bouturées s'imbriquent et font partie à présent d'un paysage unique et nouveau, celui de la Caraïbe, paysage créolisé.

Cependant, le jardinage n'est pas seulement le reflet du processus de créolisation : il est aussi l'art du colonisateur. Il existe un lien intrinsèque entre colonisation et botanique. En effet, le développement de la botanique telle qu'on la connaît aujourd'hui est le produit de l'expansion coloniale européenne. La botanique au XVIIIème siècle ne s'intéresse plus seulement aux propriétés des plantes mais surtout à leur classification. L'exploitation de la nature dans les colonies pour le profit exigeait une connaissance bien précise de cette nature : pour la maîtriser physiquement, il faut aussi la maîtriser d'un point de vue épistémique. Avec le siècle des Lumières, sa dénonciation des superstitions et du mysticisme, ses progrès scientifiques, la connaissance du monde doit être mise en œuvre par la science. Selon cette nouvelle conception du monde, la nature n'est plus à craindre ou à idolâtrer, elle est maîtrisable et au service de l'homme. Il existe ainsi des explications rationnelles des phénomènes naturels dans les livres, ou dans les catalogues : « I have a book that tells me what to do with everything in the garden » (Kincaid, 1999, p. 20).

La rationalisation de la nature s'accompagne de la création d'un système de nomenclature, celui de Linné. Carl von Linné, un botaniste suédois, met en place au XVIIIème siècle un système de nomenclature binominale pour les animaux, les végétaux et les minéraux qui s'imposera comme système officiel de classification. Ce système a pour but d'éviter d'employer les noms vernaculaires des plantes et des animaux, en les remplaçant par un binôme (c'est-à-dire bi-noms) composé d'un nom et d'un adjectif épithète. Or, comme le précise le titre d'un des chapitres de *My Garden (Book):* : « To name is to possess » (p. 114). Les puissances européennes, pour maîtriser la nature des colonies dont elles ne connaissaient rien, firent appel aux savoirs et connaissances des populations indigènes. Une fois les informations obtenues, elles ont pu être réappropriées et classées dans un système scientifique européen (Schiebinger & Swan, 2007). Il en résulte une violence épistémologique de désappropriation et de colonisation du discours environnemental, comme le soulignent DeLoughrey, Gosson et Handley (2005) : « The flora, fauna, and humans that were captured and transported lifeless to European metropoles for analysis, documentation, and display attest to the epistemic violence of the production of natural knowledge » (p. 7).

Dans ses œuvres, Kincaid pose clairement un parallèle entre colonisation et jardinage : dans les deux cas, le jardinier et le colonisateur ont un désir pour une chose lointaine, pour l'Autre, et veulent le / la posséder. Dans *Among Flowers,* Kincaid définit ainsi le jardinier : « a gardener is a person who at least once in the gardening year feels the urge to possess completely at least one plant » (p. 32). Le sentiment d'un collecteur de graines, lorsqu'il rencontre une plante rare dans la nature, est celui d'être tout-puissant : « they feel godlike, as if they had invented [it] » (pp. 32-33). Lorsqu'elle se trouve au Népal, elle admet penser essentiellement à son jardin : « How would this look in the garden? » se demande-t-elle. (p. 44). Elle prend la place de l'explorateur botaniste colonial, prend possession de la nature et se fait servir par les sherpas. Elle décrit à plusieurs reprises l'absurdité de leur faire porter tous les éléments du confort occidental. « They should bend to our demands, among which was to make us comfortable when we wanted to be comfortable. We were used to being comfortable in our native societies (Britain …; America …) » (p. 84). L'exploration prend alors une dimension économique et la narratrice semble assumer une attitude consumériste dans sa pratique du jardinage. Les plantes dans *My Garden (Book):* sont effectivement réduites à des objets de consommation que l'on commande dans un catalogue (pp. 14-15). Dans *Among Flowers,* elle considère la région himalayenne comme mystérieuse, ses jardins comme des jardins d'Eden, sa nature vierge et sauvage (p. 140).

Le jardinage est une tradition bourgeoise qui fait entièrement partie de la culture anglaise : Kincaid cite des extraits d'écrits d'auteurs anglais sur les jardins dans *My Garden (Book):,* notamment Miss Gertrude Jekyll (p. 72). Dans *Among Flowers,* le jardinage apparaît alors comme un art de maîtrise et d'appropriation de la nature : « I came to realize that the garden itself was a way of accommodating and making acceptable, comfortable, familiar, the wild, the strange » (p. 44).

Les jardins botaniques reflètent l'institutionnalisation de cette maîtrise de la nature. Ils sont les lieux de l'exposition de l'entreprise et de l'expansion coloniale. Mais ce sont aussi des lieux d'expérimentation : des greffes, des observations sur les capacités d'acclimatation des plantes sont réalisées dans les jardins botaniques de l'empire colonial. La greffe est une hybridation forcée et accélérée pour des raisons économiques et épistémiques. La greffe, et donc l'hybridation, prend alors une dimension artificielle et utilitaire : elle devient contre-nature. Avec la rationalisation des sciences, une instrumentalisation de celles-ci a été mise en place pour justifier des règles sociales. C'est ce qu'affirme Carolyn Merchant (1995):

> The scientific rationale of objectivity can legitimate
> control over whatever has been assigned by culture to
> a lower place in the "natural" order of things. It thus
> maintains a hierarchical domination of subject over
> object, male over female, and culture over nature. (p. 61)

L'hybridation dans la société est étiquetée « contre-nature », à l'image de celle que l'on opère dans des laboratoires par des procédés de greffes et de boutures. En réalité, l'hybridation et le mélange des végétaux sont des phénomènes naturels. S'opposent ainsi une hybridation accélérée, forcée, artificielle et une hybridation naturelle qui ne peut être contrôlée et que la nature réalise par elle-même. Dans la Caraïbe, la bouture est alors un phénomène artificiel, provoqué par l'homme dans le cadre de la colonisation et de la déportation, du déracinement de populations africaines, et dans celui de l'exil, n'oublions pas que Kincaid elle-même est une auteure antiguaise « transplantée » puis « bouturée » aux États-Unis. À partir de là, un processus de créolisation naturel, lent mais inévitable, s'est mis en place, mais qui se différencie de la greffe par son aspect imprévisible.

Les écrits botaniques de Kincaid sont structurés par la place paradoxale qu'occupe la narratrice : elle condamne la colonisation d'un côté, et d'un autre côté, elle semble elle-même pratiquer consciemment la maîtrise de la nature à l'image du colonisateur, peut-être dans le but de mettre en exergue ce système de domination. Cependant, ce discours reflète l'ambivalence de son rapport à la botanique. L'auteure dénonce dans *Among Flowers* l'aspect commercial du jardinage et l'absurdité d'aller collecter des graines en Himalaya et explique que les sherpas se moquent des pépiniéristes et botanistes occidentaux : « finding us and our obsession of their native plants ridiculous . . . But we had paid for this . . . » (p. 163). La gêne de la narratrice est perceptible à travers les relations que les visiteurs occidentaux entretiennent avec les populations locales, largement ignorées. À la fin de leur voyage, elle décrit l'impression que la récolte de graines ne suffit pas à exprimer leur expérience : « the impressive collection of seeds that we had made was not enough » (p. 167).

Il est intéressant de noter que Kincaid s'étonne de la possibilité de cultiver la terre sans raison particulière : ni pour se nourrir (à l'image des *provision grounds* des esclaves) ni pour des raisons de profit (à l'image des plantations de canne à sucre). Le jardinage est donc non seulement l'assouvissement d'un désir de possession, mais aussi un plaisir esthétique. Dans *Among Flowers,* Kincaid décrit les jardins d'un petit village de l'Himalaya : « Every house was surrounded by a food garden … the way they grew food, squash vines, for instance, carefully trellised and then allowed to run onto the roof of a nearby building, was so beautiful, it became a garden » (p. 65). Le jardin potager peut donc aussi acquérir une valeur artistique.

"Une éco-poétique » de la créolisation

Il est tout d'abord nécessaire d'interroger la pertinence du terme d'« éco-poétique » (Savory, 2011) ou de « poétique d'éco-relation » (Braziel, 2005, p. 110), ainsi que les liens que tisse Kincaid entre jardin et littérature. *My Garden (Book):* et *Among Flowers* portent une attention particulière à l'esthétique du jardin : Jamaica Kincaid se demande si les plantes qu'elle observe dans l'Himalaya conviendraient dans son jardin. Dans *My Garden (Book):,* il est question d'un livre de Gertrude Jekyll intitulé *Colour Schemes for the Flower Garden* : Jekyll y donne des instructions sur l'assortiment des fleurs pour que le jardinage devienne « a fine art » (p. 92). Cependant, cette rigidité esthétique ne convient pas à Kincaid, qui décide de ne pas cultiver un jardin conventionnel (comme le parterre de fleurs dans son jardin dont la forme d'archipel semble étrange à toutes les personnes qui lui rendent visite). Le jardin devient alors le reflet de son jardinier qui, comme l'écrivain, est en quête artistique du beau : « it becomes the place of great beauty which the particular gardener had in mind » (Kincaid, 1999, p. 111). Le jardin est pour le jardinier ce que le livre est pour l'écrivain. Cependant, il émane une différence notoire entre livre et jardin lorsque Kincaid affirme que le jardin meurt avec son jardinier (p. 111). Ce qui n'est pas le cas du livre, qui lui, continue d'exister sans son auteur.

L'absence totale d'autonomie du jardin par rapport à son jardinier, c'est-à-dire le contrôle que ce dernier exerce sur son œuvre doit cependant être remis en question tandis que l'on discerne une certaine imprévisibilité dans le jardin. « My garden has no serious intention, my garden has only series of doubts upon series of doubts. » (Kincaid, 1999, p. 15). Le jardinier perd la maîtrise de son œuvre : la glycine ne fleurit pas au bon moment, elle forme des tiges qui s'entremêlent aux autres plantes. Cette glycine est pour Andrée-Anne Kekeh-Dika « Une contre-figure : éloge du désordre et de l'indiscipline » (Kekeh-Dika, p. 104). La nature est incontrôlable, elle se mélange et se créolise naturellement.

Le jardinier, tout comme l'auteur, est à l'origine de son œuvre, mais la nature, comme la littérature, ne peut être rationalisée et entièrement contrôlée. Ainsi, de nombreux parallèles sont tissés entre lecture et jardinage. Kincaid s'appuie sur le jardinage pour amplifier la variété de ses lectures, et, vice versa sur ses lectures pour cultiver son art du jardinage : les deux arts sont donc liés. Elle mentionne d'ailleurs l'autorité qui se dégage des livres des botanistes : l'autorité au sens de l'influence scientifique mais aussi au sens de la production littéraire. Kincaid n'écrit-elle pas elle-même sur son activité de jardinage ? Le jardin est donc source d'inspiration pour l'écrivain, et le livre source d'inspiration pour le jardinier.

L'écrivaine met ainsi en avant le côté imprévisible de la nature, et donc la fertilité artistique du jardinage. Elle remet en cause des principes esthétiques rigides et l'idée d'une maîtrise totale de la nature. Ces remises en question passent également par celle du langage scientifique. Kincaid emploie constamment la nomenclature de Carl Von Linné. Mais tandis qu'elle l'emploie, elle l'ébranle et la discrédite : Pourquoi le *Lilium orientalis* ou « Black Beauty » n'est-il pas noir ? (p. 23) De même, elle réexamine la mise à l'écart des noms vernaculaires. Elle dit à propos de la rose de Noël ou *Christmas Rose* : « and sometimes [people] actually say *Helleborus niger*, but why? the common name sounds much better, the way common names always do » (p. 72). L'ébranlement du discours scientifique se fait également d'un point de vue poétique par la présence presque exhaustive, étouffante, envahissante des noms scientifiques (pp. 26-8). De plus, ce langage scientifique est paradoxalement mêlé à l'incertain : « Why is my *Wisteria floribunda,* trained into a standard so that it eventually will look like a small tree, blooming in late July, almost August, instead of May, the way wisterias in general are supposed to do? » (p. 11). Puis la nomenclature de Linné, précise et stable, se retrouve intégrée à une série de questions sans réponses qui ébranlent cette autorité scientifique : « What to do? . . . What should I do? What am I to do? ... And what is midsummer anyway? What should I do with such a thing? » (pp. 11-13). La poétique de Kincaid est une poétique du doute et de l'opacité : elle remet en question le langage scientifique, mais aussi le sens des mots en général et ouvre une réelle discussion sur le langage à travers la botanique. Les mots s'imprègnent d'un sens nouveau, ils ne sont plus inertes et acquièrent une certaine organicité. Kincaid écrit d'ailleurs : « the garden for me is so bound up with words about the garden, with words themselves, that any set idea of the garden, any set picture, is a provocation to me » (Kincaid, 1999, p. 7).

Le titre *My Garden (Book):* indique la superposition entre livre et jardin. Ce titre est ambivalent : s'agit-il d'un livre à propos de son jardin ou bien est-ce une manière de dire qu'elle ne sait pas comment nommer sa création, car son jardin est un livre et son livre est un jardin? Pour Andrée-Anne Kekeh-Dika, la parenthèse du titre « ouvre une double porte » puisque « l'essai est simultanément jardin et livre » (Kekeh-Dika, p. 117). La structure du livre *My Garden (Book):* est d'ailleurs comme un jardin, rythmée par les saisons : les chapitres sont intitulés « The Season Past », « Winter » et « Spring » dans la dernière section, ainsi le printemps vient à la fin, indiquant un renouveau, une certaine fertilité du livre.

Andrée-Anne Kekeh-Dika lit également la parenthèse dans le titre de *My Garden (Book):* « comme le signe d'une pénétration dans le champ du botaniste ». La parenthèse est employée dans la nomenclature botanique pour mentionner les initiales du premier botaniste à décrire l'espèce dans un genre différent. « Kincaid . . . se désigne ainsi comme l'origine et la signataire d'un ordre nouveau. Il n'y a pas de nom propre dans l'espace de la parenthèse de Kincaid contrairement à la parenthèse botanique, mais le « je » y manifeste sa présence par des apartés renvoyant sans ambiguïté à la voix énonciative qui y laisse les traces de ses doutes, questionnements ou certitudes » (Kekeh-Dika, p. 113). Les parenthèses sont pour Kincaid une autre manière de remettre en cause l'autorité de la nomenclature scientifique aux dépens des noms vernaculaires. « Ce qu'indique alors la parenthèse, c'est la possibilité pour la voix « sans nom » d'occuper un lieu de notoriété dévolu au savoir botanique et de proposer une vision modeste du monde, une voix moins péremptoire, dénuée de l'assurance et de la toute-puissance de celle qui décide de l'attribution du nom propre » (Kekeh-Dika, p. 114)

Les parenthèses sont omniprésentes et ajoutent toujours plus de sens, d'informations. Le passage ci-dessous de *My Garden (Book):* me paraît concentrer ce processus de bourgeonnement, de floraison et de créolisation du sens :

> Oh, the deliciousness of complaining about nothing of any consequence and that such a thing should be the case in a garden: because, (again) that wisteria blooming now (or then) so close to the buddleia, which in turn is not too far from the *Phlox paniculata* 'Nohr Leigh,' which is also somehow in the middle of the *Phlox paniculata* 'David,' is all pleasing to my eye, as I was looking at it then (now); at that moment of the wisteria, turning left or right (counterclockwise or clockwise), this is what I could see in front of me, this is what might be the zenith of summer in this (my) garden. (p. 22)

Ce passage met en lumière plusieurs choses : tout d'abord, visuellement, la multiplicité des parenthèses qui contiennent toujours plus de sens et se greffent au reste de la phrase pour former un sens nouveau, créolisé.

Le texte n'est pas inerte, il est vivant, organique et s'étend en un buisson d'épanorthoses : il revient constamment sur lui-même pour se corriger et ajouter du sens (lorsqu'une affirmation est jugée trop faible, il y ajoute une expression plus frappante et énergique). « Épanorthose » vient du grec *epanorthosis* (« redressement »), de orthos (« droit ») : le texte tente de se redresser, alors que celui des plantes est impossible (la glycine s'enroule dans le sens des aiguilles d'une montre ou dans le sens inverse). La parenthèse est un « lieu du non-fixe », à l'image des deux points laissés en suspens dans le titre qui « laissent entrevoir un chemin non balisé loin « des voix toutes faites » des mots » (Kekeh-Dika, p. 117).

Le passage de *My Garden (Book):* cité ci-dessus est aussi marqué par la quasi-absence de points, la longueur de la phrase et surtout les digressions constantes du texte. Son redressement est donc impossible puisque des digressions lui sont greffées en plus des épanorthoses, nous donnant l'impression que le texte s'enroule sur lui-même, à l'image des tiges de la glycine. La mention des adverbes « now » et « then » font écho à son roman *See Now Then,* comme bouturé dans *My Garden (Book):* (ou, inversement, certains passages de *My Garden (Book):* sont comme bouturés dans *See Now Then,* publié postérieurement). Le texte comporte de nombreuses répétitions, notamment celle de la question « What to do? » dont les rejets envahissent le texte. Quant à l'étymologie de « greffe », le terme vient du latin *graphium* (lui-même une dérive du verbe grec désignant l'écriture) signifiant stylet, poinçon, outils de gravure et d'écriture, faisant ainsi écho au caractère organique du texte de Kincaid dans lequel les répétitions, les références, les analepses sont florissantes tels les rejets d'une plante à partir de sa souche. Les parenthèses sont visuellement comme des rejets, de nouvelles tiges nées à partir de la phrase précédente.

Ainsi, le terme d'« éco-poétique » (Savory, 2011) de la relation caractérise bien la poétique de Kincaid dans la mesure où les mots deviennent des plantes que l'on greffe et que l'on bouture, qui se lient les uns aux autres pour former une réalité nouvelle et imprévisible qui est un texte créolisé ou se créolisant, puisque le sens n'y est pas fixé. Les textes de Kincaid sont des jardins de mots et de sens. Ils acquièrent une organicité interne qui s'étend à d'autres œuvres. Le texte, comme le jardin, est un lieu de manifestation du pouvoir et de la volonté de maîtrise de la nature, mais également un lieu de rencontre, de création, d'incertitude, de renouvellement et de créolisation.

Références

Braziel, J. E. (2011). Caribbean Genesis. Jamaica Kincaid and the Writing of New Worlds. In E. M. DeLoughrey, R. K. Gosson & G. B. Handley (Eds.). *Caribbean Literature and the Environment: Between Nature and Culture* (pp. 110-126). Albany, NY: SUNY Press.

Condé, M. (Décembre 1998). Edouard Glissant, ou les Antilles repossédées. Colloque international de New York « Edouard Glissant. De la Pensée Archipélique au Tout-Monde ».

DeLoughrey, E.M., Gosson R. K., & Handley G. B. (Eds.). (2005). *Caribbean Literature and the Environment: Between Nature and Culture.* Charlottesville, VA: University of Virginia Press.

DeLoughrey, E., and Handley, G. B. (Eds.). (2011) *Postcolonial Ecologies: Literatures of the Environment.* Oxford: Oxford University Press.

Glissant, E. (1996). *Introduction à une poétique du divers.* Paris : Gallimard.

Glissant, E. (1990). La Barque ouverte. *Poétique de la Relation.* Paris : Gallimard.

Glissant, E. (1981). *Le Discours antillais.* Paris : Seuil.

Kekeh-Dika, A. (2016). *L'Imaginaire de Jamaica Kincaid : Variations autour d'une île caraïbe.* Pessac : Presses Universitaires de Bordeaux.

Kincaid, J. (1990). *Lucy: A Novel.* New York, NY: Farrar, Straus, Giroux.

Kincaid, J. *The New Yorker.* http://www.newyorker.com/contributors/jamaica-kincaid.

Kincaid, J (1999). *My Garden (Book):.* New York, NY: Farrar, Straus, Giroux.

Kincaid, J. (2011). *Among Flowers. A Walk in the Himalaya.* Washington, D.C.: National Geographic.

Kincaid, J. (2013). *See Now Then.* New York, NY: Farrar, Straus, Giroux.

Mastnak, T., Elyachar, J., Boellstorff, T. (2014). Botanical Decolonization: Rethinking Native Plants. *Environment and Planning D Society and Space,* 32, 2, 363-380.

Merchant, C. (1995). *Earthcare: Women and the Environment.* New York, NY: Routledge.

Savory, E. (2011). Toward a Caribbean Ecopoetics: Derek Walcott's Language of Plants. In E. DeLoughrey, & G.B. Handley (Eds.), *Postcolonial Ecologies: Literatures of the Environment* (pp. 80-98). Oxford: Oxford University Press,

Schiebinger, L., & Swan, C. (Eds.). (2007). *Colonial Botany: Science, Commerce, and Politics in the Early Modern World.* Philadelphia, PA: University of Pennsylvania Press.

Stouck, J. (2005). Gardening in the Diaspora: Place and Identity in Olive Senior's Poetry. *Mosaic: A Journal for the Interdisciplinary Study of Literature,* 38, 4,103-122.

Wordsworth, W. (2004). *Selected Poems.* London: Penguin Books.

SIX

GRAPHING AND GRAFTING IN JAMAICA KINCAID'S GARDEN MEMOIRS

Josette Spartacus
Independent Scholar

Contact: josette.spartacus@gmail.com
To cite this article:
[Josette Spartacus. "Graphing and Grafting in Jamaica Kincaid's Garden Memoirs." *Wagadu: A Journal of Transnational Women's and Gender Studies,* Summer 2018, vol. 19, pp. 66-76]

Abstract

Benítez-Rojo's concepts of "plasma" and "metamachine" are at the core of this essay to understand Kincaid's foregrounding of otherness, discomfort and global underground memory in *My Garden (Book):* (1999) and *Among Flowers, A Walk in the Himalaya* (2005). Graphing and grafting become privileged metaphors for Kincaid's work as an Afro-Caribbean.

Jamaica Kincaid wrote two books on gardens, plants and flowers: *My Garden (Book):* (1999), about her first garden in Vermont, and *Among Flowers: A Walk in the Himalaya* (2005) about her trekking trip in the Himalaya with three seed collectors, in which, in Bakhtinian terms, she dialogizes gardens—not only hers but gardens all over the planet. In both books, in fact, she produces texts on plants and gardens that she dialogically infuses with a complex network of treatments, interpretations and understandings of the world as she sees it (Bakhtin, 2014). Her enterprise is aesthetically phenomenological and existentialist, as these books are works of art that both explain the historical phenomenon that started with the 'discovery' of the Americas by Christopher Columbus and reveal the impact these past events still have on the singularity of Kincaid's vision and her existence wherever she is: in Vermont or in the Himalaya. As an Afro-Caribbean and an American (*i.e.*, someone whose ancestors and herself were transplanted to different spaces at different times), she graphs what can be termed Garden Memoirs in an idiosyncratic and global sense. Indeed "grafting" and "graphing" share the same etymology: the grafting knife that was used in the Middle Ages derived its name from the late Greek and Latin words "graphium" (*i.e.*, stylus) precisely because of its resemblance to a stylus. In Kincaid's garden memoirs, the two tools (stylus and grafting knife) are bound through another intimate connection: both of them are instrumental in collecting the seeds of memory.

As such, Kincaid's garden memoirs reveal quite an unconventional vista of codes and subcodes that brings to light the world history of productions of wealth (material and cultural) in the colonial and the post-colonial worlds over the last five hundred years. Her perspective, I argue, is similar to that which is at the core of theorist Antonio Benítez-Rojo's *Repeating Island*. In his essays, Benítez-Rojo redefines Caribbean culture through a set of multiple lenses—historical, economic, sociological, psychological, religious, etc.—to interpret the essential characteristics of that region as a blend of order and disorder, two notions that are not antithetical when applied to the Caribbean. According to him, the Caribbean can be seen as ruled by a form of chaos which is both unexpected and complex but which generates unforeseen creations. The Caribbean is therefore an archipelago of paradoxes that recreates and repeats itself. Kincaid's writings exemplify Benítez-Rojo's analyses since book after book she recreates and repeats the founding experience of her Caribbean origins.

Benítez-Rojo's collection of essays on the Caribbean basin opens with a critical re-examination of Deleuze and Guattari's concept of machines, according to which desire's *primum mobile* is to initiate a chain of productions. Their theory posits desire at the center of a mechanism which enables a machine to set itself in motion, interrupt itself, then connect itself to the previous interrupter which sets another machine in motion which in turn interrupts itself only to connect itself to a third machine *etc.*, to produce a desire that repeats itself and becomes in this very process a new form of production. According to Deleuze and Guattari, when applied to the Caribbean, the device highlights how the plantation economy was interrupted and then reignited in a capitalist system which in turn connected itself to another system. This, according to Benítez-Rojo, is a post-structuralist and post-industrialist view which is inoperative in the Caribbean. He adds:

> The Caribbean machine, on the other hand, is something
> more: it is a technological-poetic machine, or, if you like,
> a metamachine of differences whose poetic mechanism
> cannot be diagrammed in conventional dimensions,
> and whose user's manual is found dispersed in a state
> of plasma within the chaos of its own network of codes
> and subcodes. (p. 18)

This dynamic is typically, I argue, what is at work in any of Kincaid's texts and these garden books in particular: they reveal to the reader a state of plasma within a chaotic network of codes and subcodes that are not only hers, but that also belong to the global world or more exactly to the unforeseen and invisible relations that connect the global world. To use Edouard Glissant's notion of *rhizome* in *The Poetics of Relation* (1990), a notion that he borrows from Deleuze and Guattari, the Caribbean can be defined through multiple identities that expand into a plurality of relationships (just like rhizomic plants that are connected thanks to their network of horizontal roots) contrary to the single, rooted, and vertical identity of the colonial world which annihilates relationship. Kincaid, I believe, weaves a rhizomic relationship with her readers through a discomforting, eclectic machine that binds their underground memory to hers. In this article I concentrate on the idiosyncrasy of the author's perspective, on the way she uses intertextuality to relate with the great number of source texts she cites, and the ontological discomfort she deliberately spurs in the reader's experience of her "gardens" to understand how her metamachine works.

Idiosyncratic Stance

Kincaid's literary approach is more often than not centered on her individual experience. When she first started gardening, she wanted flowerbeds and so had somebody dig holes in front and at the back of her house in Vermont; this was apparently so "ungardenlike" that, she realized, it triggered questions around her:

> When it dawned on me that the garden I was making (and am still making and will always be making) resembled a map of the Caribbean and the sea that surrounds it, I did not tell this to the gardeners who had asked me to explain the thing I was doing, or to explain what I was trying to do; I only marveled at the way the garden is for me an exercise in memory, a way of remembering my own immediate past, a way of getting to a past that is my own (The Caribbean Sea) and the past as it is indirectly related to me (the conquest of Mexico and its surroundings). (1999, pp. 7-8)

Kincaid isolates two poles in her idiosyncratic quest: memory and conquest. As she digs holes in her garden, a map of the Caribbean is conjured up alongside her immediate past. In the course of her gardening and writing expeditions, she understands that another past is being summoned that she has to conquer: she is confronted with the conquest of her own memory—a personal memory that is dormant, silent, unexplained and brings about existential trauma—and the memory of a conquest to which she is indirectly bound as a Caribbean subject. That second aspect of memory which is as unconscious as the other one, *i.e.*, the five hundred years that preceded her existence, demands enquiries concerning the activities of the conquering class to face the trauma of what it is to belong to the conquered. The reader has to bear in mind those two aspects—the conquest of memory (her own, in her front and back gardens) and the memory of the conquests that started with Christopher Columbus—to understand the way Kincaid dialogizes both her fiction and her garden memoirs.

As far as personal memory is concerned, "conquest" is quite straightforward: she relates the Portulaca (a flower) to a stevedore she once met, the botanical garden of Antigua to her father and her female friends, the White Head Bush to her mother (1999, p. 119). After some time spent in gardening in Vermont and doing research on the names of plants and their origins, she states: "This ignorance of the botany of the place I am from (and am of) really only reflects the fact that when I lived there, I was of the conquered class living in a conquered place" (1999, p. 120). Botany is hence a form of knowledge that she is determined to conquer, until she understands that the botanical life of Antigua as it is now, is part of a machine. The bougainvillea comes from tropical South America, the plumbago from Southern Africa, the croton from Malaysia, the hibiscus from Asia and East Africa, the allamanda from Brazil, the poinsettia from Mexico, the bird of paradise from southern Africa, the Bermuda lily from Japan, the flamboyant from Madagascar, *etc.* The list is poetically and terrifyingly vertiginous and signals a network of rhizomic conquests indeed that suddenly transforms Kincaid's book into a protest. This list exemplifies the kind of memory that Kincaid unearths through careful research. It embodies a conquest over memory and a memoir of conquests all at once.

Yet, there are times when memory works erratically. Once, as she is walking in Kew Gardens, she comes upon one of the most beautiful specimens of hollyhock, which ranks among her favorite flowers. When looking at the label she discovers that it is not a hollyhock at all but a Gossypium, whose common name is cotton. This provokes the following reflection: "Cotton all by itself exists in perfection ... but the tormented, malevolent role it has played in my ancestral history is not forgotten by me. Even so, long after its role in the bondage of some of my ancestors had been eliminated, it continued to play a part in my life" (1999, p. 150). This incident triggers a long trail of memories related to her childhood in Antigua where she had to pick cotton at one of her mother's friends' place during the summer holidays. It was a fastidious job which made her hands sore. The details she (Jamaica Kincaid, the writer, not a character in a fiction, not even a botanist) gives of this past event are so vivid that she feels the urge to add: "This is not a fiction" (1999, p. 151). This is both a conquest over her own memory (the little girl picking cotton) and a memory of conquests (the gossypium / cotton which conquered the Americas and her ancestors).

But, of course, the reverse of the coin is that the expertise that she acquires in terms of conquest over memory and memory of conquests makes her part of the conquerors. Or perhaps she was idiosyncratically so to start with. The confession is actually hers: "I have joined the conquering class: who else could afford this garden—a garden in which I grow things that it would be much cheaper to buy at the store? My feet are (so to speak) in two worlds" (1999, p. 123). And the 'rest' follows: the craving for possession (in her case the possession of seeds and plants), the naming of things, the desire to kill whatever does not behave in her garden (a wisteria on page 13, rabbits, slugs) and the compulsion to scour the world (the U.S., Europe, China, the Himalaya). This feature was already present in her trilogy *Annie John, Lucy*, and *The Autobiography of My Mother*, culminating in this last novel in which Xuela is taking possession of herself, scouring the island and the whole Caribbean archipelago in a trance-like dream, killing a turtle, then a dog and naming the world in English instead of Creole as a four-year old child. Remarkably, in *The Autobiography of My Mother*, she is not mourning her mother but is at last free to give birth to herself, without the sufferings of a mother (and also far from a problematically emasculated colonial father figure). The graphing is scathing and again, complex and unexpected: Kincaid grafts onto the Caribbean discourse a new idiosyncratic vision whereby one could literally kill to be born again and stop numbering among the conquered.

The repetition of the conqueror's act of possessing is further developed in her garden memoirs, especially when, in *Among Flowers*, the author states:

> a gardener is a person who at least once in the gardening year feels the urge to possess at least one plant. ... You can hear this form of possession in the voice of someone who will utter a sentence like this: "I saw some Codonopsis growing up there, couldn't tell which one it was but I took the seeds anyway." ... The person who says such a sentence is in a complicated state of craving ... they feel godlike. (2005, p. 32)

Kincaid is supposedly not in that godlike position; in this excerpt she merely witnesses the phenomenon as an outsider. As a gardener, however, she faces the same predicament as the gardeners she depicts. She is equally overwhelmed by an urge to possess plants as she anxiously waits for the catalogues of her favorite plant nurseries. She is therefore both an outsider and an insider, in a position of in-betweenness that structures her entire literary enterprise. As she repeatedly focuses on the symptoms of the conquered and the conquerors, her Garden Memoirs prove she is both. Hence, being in two worlds, she creates a new space where her writings relate to her readers in a rhizomic way, which is in keeping with Glissant's concept, at the same time as they signal a paradox producing a new form of creation: Benítez-Rojo's repeating island.

Intertextuality: Kincaid's Conquest over Graphing

When Kincaid first started to dig holes in her back garden in Vermont, she was (unconsciously?) addressing the essence of her "poetic-technological machine," to use Benítez-Rojo's term. Kincaid's machine is resonant with the machine in the "The Ancient Mariner" as the Ancient Mariner is not only compulsively repeating his ballad to passersby but also repeating lines to incrementally extend them with the details of his traumatic adventure. Each stanza contains a repeated line and is further augmented with the fearsome elements of his story, which gradually reinforce the depth of his trauma on the reader/ listener's mind. Kincaid's technique is thus akin to the ballad form, whose haunting trope is incremental repetition, as shown by Kincaid's account of how the garden started in *My Garden (Book):*. If one believes Kincaid's account, her garden started with a hole and a book:

> This is how my garden began; then again, it would not be at all false to say that just at that moment I was reading a book and that book (written by the historian William Prescott) happened to be about the conquest of Mexico, or New Spain, as it was then called, and I came upon the flower called . . . zinnia, and after that the garden was to me more than the garden as I used to think of it. (1999, p. 6)

This confession appears at the very beginning of *My Garden (Book):* and it is only halfway through the book that the reader has the explanation of such a cryptic sentence, at the same time as the explanation of the appearance of the Caribbean archipelago in Kincaid's garden. The name of William H. Prescott is repeated, and so is the title of his book, but what is added is the story of the dahlia. The original name of the dahlia in Mexico was "cocoxichitl," it was "conquered" there, then sent to Europe where a Swedish botanist, Andreas Dahl, renamed it. Andreas Dahl was the pupil of Carolus Linnaeus, another Swede, who invented the binomial system of naming plants. This is information that

Kincaid gathers from another book: *The Oxford Companion to Gardens*, which she says she often wants to hurl across the room, so full is it of prejudice (p. 121). This train of thought leads her to note:

> This naming of things is so crucial to possession –
> a spiritual padlock with the key thrown irretrievably
> away – that it is a murder, an erasing, and it is not
> surprising that when people have felt themselves prey
> to it (conquest), among their first acts of liberation is
> to change their names (Rhodesia to Zimbabwe, LeRoi
> Jones to Amiri Baraka). (1999, p. 122)

She does not share the example of her own name change (from Elaine Cynthia Potter Richardson to Jamaica Kincaid) but the fact is that we are back to something that repeats itself: the conquest, the loss, the naming and the graphing of the loss. Kincaid uses a vast number of texts, magazines, catalogues, dictionaries, history books, novels to graph her own vision of what should be grafted in her own ideal garden and what should be discarded or ferociously cut off, like the wisteria that did not behave (1999, p. 113). Hence an excerpt from Henry James's *The Portrait of a Lady* (1999, p. 114) is discarded on the grounds that it is redolent of the conquering class, and Vita Sackville-West's garden writing is declared too oblivious of how "the world cannot be left out of the garden" (1999, p. 82). She sees an excerpt from a novel by Tsitsi Dangarembga as the epitome of what personal *liberation* means (1999, p. 116): planting for joy when previous and present generations had been planting for a living, and when that work had been torture. Writing about such a revelation in the midst of contradictory strategies of survival seems to be the appropriate aesthetic gesture for Kincaid: a seed to be planted in her own library.

In the end, most of the intertexts that Kincaid deploys in *My Garden (Book):* point to one issue: we, readers, are in a narrative because we belong to a Western world that is not new and that repeats itself, like the garden with its plants conquered all over the planet and renamed within a binomial system invented by Carolus Linnaeus, who wrote a document of this narrative. Here is what Kincaid says:

> The invention of this [binomial] system has been a good thing. Its narrative would begin in this way: In the beginning, the vegetable kingdom was chaos, people everywhere called the same things by a name that made sense to them, not by a name arrived at by an objective standard. But who has an interest in an objective standard? Who needs one? It makes me ask again, What to call the thing that happened to me and all who look like me? Should I call it history? And if so, what should history mean to someone who looks like me? Should it be an idea; should it be an open wound, each breath I take in and expel healing and opening the wound again, over and over, or is it a long moment that begins anew each day since 1492? (1999, p. 166).

Hence, her awareness of the loss of so many memories since 1492 reactivates the chaos and plasma that Benítez-Rojo discusses. One also has to bear in mind that all these intertexts point to Kincaid's scientific method. For example, in *My Garden (Book):* before she sets on a journey to China with a dozen plant collectors, she explains:

> A journey like this, for someone like me, begins in so many ways: in a book by the plant hunter Frank Kingdon-Ward, *Plant Hunting on the Edge of the World,* an account of his travels looking for plants in China; a book by Ernest Wilson, *Plant Hunter's Paradise,* an account of his travels looking for plants in China; a book by Patrick Synge, *Mountains of the Moon,* an account of his travels looking for plants in Africa; a book by Reginald Farrer, *Among the Hills,* an account of his travels in the Alps looking for alpine plants. (1999, p. 190)

Many other volumes are listed in the two garden books—some of them history books, novels, essays, *etc.*—apart from the catalogues and the dictionaries. They form and inform the researcher and the memory collector that Kincaid is. This is not fiction indeed, but a body of knowledge she has to appropriate and master, almost in an encyclopedic mode (just like the Latin denominations of plants and flowers that Linneaus spent his life encoding encyclopedically) to master and to push forward the seriousness and the universal directionality of her quest. After she has hoarded such knowledge, the author can afford to stand her ground. In China, as she is on a seed-gathering expedition, a plant collector named John insults her by saying she is always "bitchin' and bitchin'" (1999, p. 207). She turns this into a badge of honor, saying: "If a person who stroked his beard and caressed his nose was against bitching, then most certainly a person like me must be a bitch" (1999, p. 208). Kincaid does not spare her reader either. She draws her into her own ontological discomfort: one that is both physical and intellectual. The author has already noted that reading for her—like gardening—is a physical activity. She says that gardening and reading are the two things she loves best and she must have the two (1999, p. 78), adding, "I read my books, but I also *use* them; that is, sometimes the reading is almost a physical act" (1999, p. 81, italics in the original). There are allusions to the smell of her body when she has been gardening a whole day and allusions to the exertions and functions of the body when she is trekking in China and the Himalaya. The reader is therefore taken into an adventure which is historical, botanical, intellectual, physical, and sensual. It is a complex experience which involves the body and the mind whereby the reader can unearth her own discomfort.

Ontological Discomfort and Otherness

Kincaid concentrates on her discomfort. Both her Caribbean origins and her compulsive stance as a gardener drive her scientifically to describe the ontological phenomenon that triggered the object of her existential discomfort. Her approach is therefore by essence scientific, since it aims to decipher the core reality and origins of the object of her discomfort.

In her garden memoirs, the "object" is plants. What she finds is a chasm between ontological discomfort and existential questioning.

In *Among Flowers* discomfort seems to be less acute than in *My Garden (Book):. My Garden (Book):* teems with questions: "What to do?" "What should I do?" "Should I call this History?" "What is a wild garden?" "How should I feel?" "Where should I place myself?" (1999, pp. 153/166). At the source of these questions for Kincaid as a Caribbean, there is a date, 1492, when Christopher Columbus first landed in the West Indies. 1492 signals the starting point of her trauma and her discomfort. This discomfort is ontological because it encapsulates the essence of her being, it is part and parcel of her DNA, a metaphorical seed planted in the Antiguan soil in 1492 which historically, sociologically, and "plasmatically", rhizoming out into Kincaid's own existence centuries afterwards. Hence, at the source of the questions she asks herself, there is an island, Antigua. Paradoxically, there is also the garden in Vermont which is a place where she can at last "come inside" and allow the questioning to arise but also thoughts of doom and life: "Walking around the garden, then, I am full of thoughts of doom, I am full of thoughts of life beyond my imagining. I come inside" (1999, p. 61). In a word, the "coming inside" starts the ontological research. The outside/ inside movement as much as the in-betweenness trope exposed earlier generate meaning.

Doom and thoughts of life are part and parcel of her ontological discomfort. This point has been developed by critic Patricia Donatien under the apt phrasing of "exorcism of the wound" (*L'exorcisme de la blès*). Whatever mastery Kincaid can acquire through her rumination over the loss of memory, and world machinery, that started in 1492, discomfort is lurking at every corner of her graphing expedition. As she says on page 224: "A gardener, any gardener, is not a stable being; That gardener, any gardener, is not a model of consistency" (1999, p. 224). Perhaps also because a garden does not behave. While she "first came to the garden with practicality in mind, a real beginning that would lead to a real end" (1999, p. 219), she had to acknowledge that a garden leads to no end. It has a beginning: it had one for Kincaid in Vermont a decade or so before, and it had another one for the Caribbean and the global world from 1492 onwards; but the process proved unending. What is a wild garden then? The prototype Kincaid has in mind is of course the Garden of Eden, with a tree of life and a tree of knowledge. We all know the story which Kincaid graphs this way: "Is this Eden, that thing that was banished, turned out into the world as I have come to know it—the world of discarding only to reclaim, of rejecting and then claiming again, the world of such longing that its end (death) is a relief?" (1999, p. 222). In this particular instance, Kincaid grafts rather than *writes* since The Supreme Gardener had written the story of Eden that cannot be rewritten. The graphium/stylus remains therefore the appropriate human tool when Eden is no longer an option.

So, what to do? By the end of *My Garden (Book):* Kincaid puts forward an idiosyncratic answer: "Eden is like that, so rich in comfort, it tempts me to cause discomfort; I am in a state of constant discomfort and I like this state so much I would like to share it" (p. 229), which she does with a perfect mastery of her stylus. *Among Flowers,* the story of her trek in the Himalayan mountains with three plant collectors, offers a more slanted view, if only for two reasons, both related to physicality and corporeality. The four hikers/collectors have to walk through areas infested with leeches that suck their blood, climb steep mountainous slopes in drastic conditions, sleep sometimes literally on rocks, and eat whatever is available; yet they walk on day after day to reach their destination. The book tackles the experience of being faced with an arduous mountainous environment where time and distances are flimsy notions and where the body itself becomes the basic *tool* to understand, capture, dialogize whatever sits inside and outside. In these drastic conditions, Kincaid very often finds herself lagging behind her trekking companions and she explains:

> And my difficulties were these: I found each plant, each
> new turn in the road, each new turn in the weather,
> from cold to hot and then back again, each new set

of boulders so absorbing, so new, and the newness so
absorbing, and I was so in need of an explanation for
each thing, that I was often in tears, troubling myself
with questions, such as what am I and what is the thing
in front of me. (2005, p. 135)

It seems that the writer is coming to terms here with the notion of the
wild garden, a moment of reckoning that is also most probably cathartic.
She is no longer confronted with History, memory or conquest as in her
book on her garden in Vermont: rather, the discomfort experienced in
those few lines surges from the "novelty" of the wild environment. She
cannot connect this "new" garden to anything (in her story or History
at large) which had contributed to mold her as a person. Hence the
question "what (and not "who") am I." Before this wild garden, she
is naked (a new Eve?) and is faced not so much with an ontological
discomfort as with some existential one.

The second reason for her discomfort is the marauding presence of the
Maoists. They could be seen as a repeating symptom of violence and
conquest, which they are, but more intrinsically they are the symptoms
of death, including the death of dreams. When the three seed collectors
and Kincaid have almost completed their journey, they reach a village
called Donje, where the Maoists appear not as a mere background threat
but as a physical, actual presence: they are belligerent and loud, and ask
the whole village to sit down for a lecture that lasts the whole afternoon.
Meanwhile, the plant collectors start cleaning the seeds they had just
been collecting and she writes:

Perhaps that moment is one of many that holds in it a
metaphor of the very idea of the garden itself: we had
in our possession seeds, that, if properly germinated,
would produce some of the most beautiful and desirable
flowering plants to appear in a garden situated in the
temperate zone; at the very same time we were in danger
of being killed and our dream of the garden in the

> temperate zone, the place in which we lived, would die
> with us also. At the very moment we were projecting
> ourselves into an ideal idyll we were in between life and
> death. (2005, p. 169)

The ideal idyll (the Garden of Eden) is recalled and becomes "discomforting" since it was also the symptom of a displacement for Adam and Eve, away from the "dream of the garden" as they conceived it.

In these two books—which were not conceived as a diptych—Kincaid creates for her reader a dynamic discomfort, a sense of in-betweenness which is nonetheless echoed from *My Garden (Book):* to *Among Flowers* and in reverse: between inside and outside, between graphing and grafting, between the past and the present, between Antigua and the rest of the world, between the garden in Vermont and the Himalaya, between the tree of life and the tree of knowledge. This movement through graphing is disquieting: it is akin to the criss-cross pattern analyzed by Andrée-Anne Kekeh-Dika (2016, p. 22) in her work on Jamaica Kincaid, which suggests that writing codes and reading codes have to be continually reassessed. At the center point of these skills and strategies lies the *desire* of relationship. Criss-crossing writing was a practice that imposed itself throughout the nineteenth century in letter writing, very often between relatives: the blank page that was folded into an envelope and sealed, forced the authors of such letters to write horizontally and diagonally, thus saturating the space with information whose meanings had to be decoded by the recipient of the letter. This graphing and decoding demanded a kaleidoscopic, rhizomic, creative, relation-based insight which was not binomial (as Carolus Linnaeus opined in the early eighteenth century).

Hence Kincaid, whose writings are more often than not self-centered, idiosyncratic, disobedient, and written against the grain of convenient clichéd images, presents her readers with a kaleidoscopic vision that is initially hers but ends up being theirs. The experience is all the more discomforting in *My Garden (Book):* and in *Among Flowers,* as it was precisely what she wanted to share, what she actually had warned her reader about: Eden had never been the right place to be as a human being. The graphing of this experience on gardens is intimate but turns out to be collective. It is a world machine that was grafted centuries ago by the Western world. Yet, what is also revealed contrapuntally in those texts are a series of existential and essential questions: what are *we* readers, and what are these things in front of us? These are the questions that Kincaid asks: the answers are to be collected here and there, they are unstable yet rhizomic. They rhizome from Antigua to Vermont to the world at large and graft themselves onto the reader's memory.

References

Bakhtin, M. M. (2014). *The Dialogic Imagination. Four Essays.* (C. Emerson & M. Holquist, Trans.). Austin, TX: University of Texas Press. (Original work published 1958)

Benítez-Rojo, A. (2001). *The Repeating Island. The Caribbean and the Postmodern Perspective.* (J.E Maraniss, Trans.). Second Edition. Durham, NC and London: Duke University Press. Original work published 1989)

Deleuze, G. & Guattari, F. (1972). *L'Anti-Œdipe. Capitalisme et schizophrénie.* Paris: Editions de Minuit.

Deleuze, G. & Guattari, F. (1980). *Mille Plateaux. Capitalisme et schizophrénie 2.* Paris: Editions de Minuit.

Donatien-Yssa, P. (2007). *L'Exorcisme de la blès, vaincre la souffrance dans* Autobiographie de ma mère de Jamaica Kincaid. Paris: Le Manuscrit.

DuBois, W. E. B. (2012). *The Souls of Black Folk.* New York, NY: Signet. (First published 1903)

Gilroy, P. (1993). *The Black Atlantic, Modernity and Double Consciousness.* Cambridge, MA: Harvard University Press.

Glissant, E. (1990). *Poétique de la Relation.* Paris: Gallimard.

Kekeh-Dika, A-A. (2016). *L'imaginaire de Jamaica Kincaid. Variations autour d'une île caraïbe.* Pessac: Presses Universitaires de Bordeaux.

Kincaid, J. (1985). *Annie John.* New York, NY: Farrar, Straus and Giroux.

Kincaid, J. (1990). *Lucy.* New York, NY: Farrar, Straus and Giroux.

Kincaid, J. (1997). *The Autobiography of my Mother.* New York, NY: Plume Books.

Kincaid, J. (1999). *My Garden (Book):.* New York, NY: Farrar, Straus and Giroux.

Kincaid, J. (2005). *Among Flowers: A Walk in the Himalaya.* Washington, DC: National Geographic.

SEVEN

THE GLOBALISED GARDEN: JAMAICA KINCAID'S POSTCOLONIAL GOTHIC

Eleanor Byrne
Manchester Metropolitan University

Contact:
Eleanor Byrne, Manchester Metropolitan University
e.byrne@mmu.ac.uk

To cite this article:
[Eleanor Byrne. "The Globalised Garden: Jamaica Kincaid's Postcolonial Gothic." *Wagadu: A Journal of Transnational Women's and Gender Studies,* Summer 2018, vol. 19, pp. 77-90]

Abstract

This article examines the tension between the pleasures of gardening and the colonial legacy of botany in Jamaica Kincaid's *My Garden (Book):* arguing that her work involves an uncanny worlding that haunts the present, speaks of forgotten violences and demonstrates a common ground between vegetal, animal and human lives in the Anthropocene.

Plant Thinking

Are plants doomed to self effacement as perpetual stand-ins for something else be it the material basis of industrial development or romantic love? How can literature disentangle life from its symbolic means and 'go back to the plants themselves'? Michael Marder & Patricia Vieira (2013, p. 44)

Jamaica Kincaid's dialogue with the landscape of the garden in *My Garden (Book):* (1999) and her account of searching for seeds in Nepal in *Among Flowers: A Walk in the Himalaya,* (2005) involve a confrontation with the perpetual "standing-in" for other things of plants themselves. Her writing on plants is marked by a profound ambivalence, both an enthusiasm for being a gardener and a constant negotiating with botanical history. The thoughts of a postcolonial writer and gardener whose reflections on the relation between human and plant extend to explore the legacies of the globalised movement of plants might be termed a kind of "plant thinking": a thinking with and about plants in which a kind of vegetal thought narrates the haunting of what I will argue is a globalised gothic garden. I have borrowed the term "plant thinking" from the philosopher Michael Marder's extensive and fascinating work on plant life in philosophy and poetry. In *The Philosopher's Plant* (2013), Marder explores the workings of a particular plant on the thinking of philosophers throughout Western history, discussing the little acknowledged presence of plants and trees in philosophical thought, with offerings such as Heidegger's Apple Tree, Hegel's Grapes and Kant's Tulip. These short essays enable Marder to argue for a series of philosophical failings around thinking with or about plants, where "plants themselves have been forlorn as they were supposed to point to a reality beyond themselves, ranging from Ideas to Spirit. The forgetting of the growing trees, herbs, or flowers corresponds to and stems from the forgetting of being in the midst of various attempts to name it" (p. 39). By examining a single plant and its role in the thought of an established philosopher he creates ways of teasing out and deconstructing the founding concepts on which different concepts rest.

In their essay "Writing Phytophilia: Philosophers and Poets as lovers of Plants" (2013) where Marder and Patricia Vieira trace the role of plants in Rousseau's philosophy and the profession of a "love" of plants in Western Metaphysics, they comment: "with very few exceptions metaphysical philosophers have not been phytophiles and so were incapable of loving being as a whole" (p. 39). They suggest that Rousseau was one of the few, who referred to himself as a botanophile:

> Rousseau's love of plants was not the product of a naïve yearning to abolish the distance that separates humanity corrupted by civilization from nature. This would be impossible, as Derrida notes in *Of Grammatology*, both signification and representation are supplements of presence which they actually constitute investing it with meaning – as such these supplements could be trimmed down or brought back in touch with their purportedly natural foundations but never completely eliminated. (p. 39)

Their problem is "how to resist on the one hand the metaphysical instrumentalization of the flora and on the other hand its fetishizing mystification" (p. 39). Rousseau's love of plants requires an attempt to see them as they truly are, not to impose anthropocentric ways of reading or using plants. "Rousseau passionately desires to lose himself 'like an insect' among the grasses of the meadows, being true to plants would be a kind of melting into the world, a certain detachment from the self then, a depersonalisation, that tries to see the plant as it really is, whilst acknowledging this can't even really happen" (p. 39).

As they acknowledge, plants "as such" will forever elude us as our understanding of their being is necessarily mediated through human senses and perception, scientific knowledge and the long cultural history of human vegetal interaction. It is this uncanny eluding that I would argue characterises Kincaid's struggle to think the significance of her relation to the plants she tends and attempts to nurture, as well as the plants that interfere in different ways with her thinking. In the spirit of Marder and Vieira's association of specific plants with particular philosophical modes I would propose a productive reading might be made of the significance of a number of plants in *My Garden (Book):* (1999), in very different locations: the Wisteria in her Vermont garden, the Breadfruit Tree, and the Rubber Tree in the glass house in the Botanical Garden in Antigua. Whilst there are many moments of reflection alongside different plants in her text that are also discussed for example, these represent two differing dynamics and trajectories. They point to the tension in trying to see plants as they really are, in the face of supplementary forms of representation and signification that mark human-plant interactions. Opening with a discussion of Wisteria and closing with an account of the Breadfruit and the Rubber Tree this discussion will reflect on Kincaid's exploration and archaeology of entangled histories of nature.

The Wisteria, which features in the opening chapter of the book, offers an anxious and excited gardener a chance to contemplate the wilfulness and incomprehensibility of nature. Kincaid's account of her excitement as a new gardener is immersive and overwhelming:

> Oh, how I like the rush of things, the thickness of things, everything condensed as it is happening, long after it has happened, so that any attempt to understand it will become like an unravelling of a large piece of cloth that had been laid flat and framed and placed as a hanging on a wall and, even then, expected to stand for something. (p. 24)

The image is that of a mesh, interconnected and inscrutable, coloured by images of thickness and condensation, which Kincaid embraces precisely because there is a pleasure in this incomprehensibility. The

Wisteria eludes Kincaid, it appears to have a mind of its own, to flower at the "wrong" time and to upset her knowledge of gardening. Kincaid's response to this unreadability of the Wisteria is the repeated refrain "what to do?" When Kincaid asks "What should I do? What am I to do?" there is a pleasure in the inability to decide how best to respond to something out of her own control. She comments, "how agitated I am when I am in the garden, and how happy I am to be so agitated … Nothing works the way I thought it would, and nothing looks the way I had imagined it" (p. 14). Whilst the Wisteria remains inscrutable and defeats her own desire for control and authority, the delight of engaging with the plant on its own terms as unknowable and answering to another mode of existing is intensely enjoyable. Kincaid's account of this experience is resonant with Marder and Vieira's comments: "The inaccessibility of plant life does not mean we should relinquish attempts to relate to plants on their own grounds—even to learn from their specific mode of existence. What is it like to be a plant, imagination is a vital entry point into the lives of plants" (p. 40). For Kincaid the garden is filled with awe, and whilst practical gardening has a role to play, it is doubts, amazement and awe that are the true gifts of the garden: "I know the practical, it will keep you breathing; awe, on the other hand, is what makes you (me) want to keep living" (1999, p. 16).

However, if the opening chapter is a paean to the strangeness and otherness of plant life, subsequent chapters in the book reflect on the multiple ways in which historical legacies of violent transplantation, radically transformed landscapes, offer a drastic intervention in the potential of Kincaid to think with, or through, plants.

The Globalized Garden

> I am not in nature. I do not find the world furnished like a room, with cushioned seats and rich-coloured rugs. To me, the world is cracked, unwhole, not pure, accidental; and the idea of moments of joy for no reason is very strange (p. 124).

Jamaica Kincaid's garden writing might be understood as offering a way to explore some of the current cultural and historical dynamics that make up what Rob Wilson (2007) calls "uncanny world dwelling" as she deliberates on the ethics of "taking care" and the uncanny effects of "making the world horizon come near" through acts of disorienting imagining in the globalised garden (p. 217). In such a reading we could approach Jamaica Kincaid's *My Garden (Book):* as a text that might be drawn into a broader canon of postcolonial ecocritical literatures, thinking through the role of writing about plants as a vital part of Kincaid's writing life. *My Garden (Book):* is an act of earth remembering but is fraught with pitfalls and a kind of emotional repulsion from the history that accompanies the pleasures of tending plants so significant to Kincaid as a gardener. This essay will ask if we might go further and see Kincaid's archaeology of plant histories as a kind of thinking with and through plants, where vegetal life is narrated in ways that enable the Anthropocene to come into view.

It is potentially a risky endeavour to apply a set of themes conceived in (over)developed nations to those postcolonial locations where other histories and ways of resisting imperialist power have developed. There is as, DeLoughrey *et. al.* (2005) note, a long history of cultural and ideological mismatches between first and third worlds where intellectual imperialism is enacted by academics in other places, only too familiar with imperialist methodologies, blind spots, wilful amnesia and outright denial, of the previous histories and power relations. It is with this concern that they ask whether the emerging field of ecocriticism can be brought into dialogue with Caribbean writing whilst being mindful of the contradictions and pitfalls of such a project. As the introduction stresses, they are alert to accusations of "grafting" ecocriticism onto the Caribbean, offering a critique of the introverted focus of North American ecocriticism as it was then taking hold in the academy. The essays in the collection propose to take up the challenge to move ecocriticism beyond nature writing, acknowledging the very serious ideological difficulties of seeking critical insights through ecocriticism as it then manifested. In "Worlding as Future Tactic" Wilson (2007) argues that the study of culture in the era of globalisation involves exploring how reading "texts of contemporary being and uncanny world dwelling can become a historical process of taking care and setting limits, entering into and making the world horizon come near, and become local and informed, situated and instantiated as an uneven/incomplete process of world becoming" (p. 217). Wilson comments further,

> Our own time of world globalisation is a destitute time in which the man of capitalogic has all but forgotten the nature of being, the very worlding processes of 'dwelling' or 'building up' and 'worlding'. Caring for literature and the humanities in this oblivious time of Earth forgetting can become an ex-static way of attending to language as a site of the historically determinate disclosure of the world horizon as such. (p. 216)

One area that might fruitfully be explored is the rise in postcolonial gothic and tropical gothic that has recently considered the ways in which Oceanic and Caribbean landscapes are haunted by buried traumas of invasion and genocide that underpin unsettled settling and bear witness to buried or disavowed histories of the planation culture, resource extraction that were and still are the machines of the colonial and imperialist project. Arguing for the term "tropical gothic," Justin D. Edwards and Sandra G. Vasconcelos migrate the term from its usual geographical domiciles, to suggest tropical gothic works to "tropicalize" the gothic, such that it performs with an intercultural and bidirectional dynamic, by reviving gothic images and themes in ways that mobilise and reuse dominant gothic tropes (2016). The concept of circulating images and tropes rather than the transfer or expansion of them is vital, if one is not to reduce this to a structure that reiterates unidirectional flows from centre to margins. Rather the postcolonial writer might be seen to deploy gothic as a mode of interrogating the silences of the present or of official histories.

Where the effects of globalisation and postcolonial experiences of violences done to self, nation and land converge or collide with intimations of globalised ecological catastrophe, further gothic forms proliferate. It is unsurprising, then, that ecogothic literature and criticism have arisen out of what Jason Moore (2015) terms the "world ecology" of wealth, power and nature of global capitalism—where ecological thinking is absent or repressed and the gothic is a culturally significant point of contact between criticism, postcolonial and ecocritical theory. Coming from a different critical space, we might also be able to read this form of de-distancing as a kind of unnatural or unsettling grafting, any kind of connecting up that unsettles distances between things or categories, which results in a changed perspective on the world. One such space where this seems to chime with contemporary ecocritical thought is the work of Timothy Morton, whose work on uncanny extreme intimacy also addresses the difficulties that attend to thinking globally about a localised vision or experience. In *Dark Ecology* (2016) he comments:

> when massive entities such as the human species and global warming become thinkable they grow near. They are so massively distributed we can't directly grasp them empirically. We vaguely sense them growing out of the corner of our eye while seeing the date in the centre of our vision. These hyperobjects remind us that the local is in fact uncanny. (p. 11)

Isn't Kincaid's garden haunted after all? The garden is full of death, the woodpecker and the robins are poisoned, the house walls are being attacked, rabbits are invaders and Kincaid fantasises about killing them. Death stalks the garden, despite its association with nurture, and the garden itself must be made from the ruins of the garden that went before. Kincaid comments, "every garden dies with the gardener" and she is meticulous in her memorialisation of the previous owners of the house and their gardening, as she narrates her own labours, refusing to be seen to be working on a "blank" or empty space, acknowledging the lives and work that have preceded her own occupation of house and land. In her introduction to *My Garden (Book):*, Kincaid recounts the origins of her creation of a garden from the remains of what had been left by the previous owner in her Vermont home, alongside her attempts to learn about horticulture. Asserting that every garden has a history, in her opening chapter, Kincaid recounts her earliest attempt to do something she thinks of as gardening. She takes her garden to be a blank, empty canvas, and she has paid a gardener to regrade the lawn of a house she has moved into and whose previous owner, McGovern, has died. Soon after she sees a series of maroon leaf sprouts pushing up in patches across the lawn and she is considering complaining about the job done in her garden to the neighbour who kindly points out that this is not a "lawn problem" but the shoots of peonies that Kincaid had no knowledge of. The uncanny sprouting of the previous owner's flowers from the ground beneath the overlaid lawn, points to the garden as palimpsest that an amateur gardener/reader cannot fully navigate. There will always be unburyings, uncanny interruptions of a controlled or overlaid new landscape, where a history of concealed actions and traces of others' lives still remain deep in the soil, that may reveal themselves, uncannily, not uninvited guests to the property, not invaders, but ghosts, original or preceding inhabitants, introduced to the garden by other owners and gardeners, whose legacy must be reckoned with. This opening up of the garden to being something other than itself "beside itself," stages the garden as having "always already" been uncanny. To an extent Kincaid hangs onto these legacies, stating that she was "firmly living in Mrs. McGovern's house (or the Yellow House, which is what the children came to call it . . .)" (pp. 6-7), as if the previous owner were merely hosting her.

If the garden is uncanny it is because the previous owner of the land has the ability to "return" through her plants. But it is not just the local ghosts of past owners that haunt. Kincaid's garden is full of colonial ghosts, brought to mind through the naming of plants. This is suggestive of a ghoulish grafting of colonial explorers' names onto the plants in the garden that conjures the ghosts of these explorers and their missions, as if their heads had been grafted on to stems where flowers should be. Bougainville looms over the garden, the legacy of his circumnavigation of the world written into every pink blossom. His voyage, which was the first by a Frenchman, was also the first to take naturalists and geographers aboard, which enabled his claim to a plant named after him by the naturalist Philibert Commerçon. Facing the garden and learning about plants is also a confrontation with other histories:

> It would not be at all false to say that just at that moment I was reading a book and that book (written by the historian William Prescott) happened to be about the conquest of Mexico, or New Spain, as it was then called, and I came upon a flower called marigold, and the flower called dahlia and the flower called zinnia, and after that the garden was to me more than the garden as I used to think of it. After that the garden was also something else. (Kincaid, 1999, p. 6)

It appears that the historian of plants cannot fail to unearth stories of colonial devastation and appropriation that intrude onto the illusory peacefulness of the flower garden. It produces a double vision, looking with two eyes, one phenomenological and one semiotic, where the garden is at once raw, alive and corporeal, timeless and also where all is a sign, a code that leads to a vertiginous dizzying set of unfolding and unending narratives of conquest, exploitation and disaster. Kincaid must trouble the archive of gardening, and rail against its complicity with the colonial underpinning of gardening itself: "*The Oxford Companion to Gardens* (a book I often want to hurl across the room, it is so full of prejudice)" (p. 121). She comments, "the garden for me is so bound up with words about the garden, with words themselves, that any set idea of the garden, any set picture, is a provocation to me" (p. 7).

Kincaid's text suggests that the gardener needs to develop a competence in "reading," orienting themselves as with a key to a map, in order to navigate the meaning of the plants in the garden. Kincaid notes that the names of plants perform a historical assault on her as a Caribbean gardener, even in Vermont, "One day, while looking at the things that lay at my feet, I was having an argument with myself over the names I should use when referring to the things that lay before me. These things were plants. The plants, all of them—and there were hundreds—had two names" (p. 160). In that it signals the complex intertwining of the violent histories of forced transplantation and settlement, human, and botanic, that render the landscape of the Caribbean as Wilson Harris states, "a landscape saturated by traumas of conquest' (1962, p. 8). Kincaid reflects on this as she makes her own garden and comes to the realisation that she has produced a map of the Caribbean. She continues:

> I do not tell this to the gardeners who had asked me to try to explain the thing I was doing, or to explain what I was trying to do; I only marvelled at the way the garden is for me an exercise in memory, a way of remembering my own immediate past, a way of getting to a past that is my own (the Caribbean Sea) and the past as it is indirectly related to me (the conquest of Mexico and its surroundings). (p. 8)

In this apprehension Kincaid is paradigmatic of DeLoughrey *et al.*'s thoughts about the ways in which "the history of transplantation and settlement have contributed to a sense of place and an environmental ethic in the Caribbean" (2005, p. 135). Kincaid's meditation on the demands to think through how the ruins of extractive colonialism and plantation culture can be lived in the present shares Antonio Benítez-Rojo's (1996) assertions that living in the wake of colonial botanical histories means that "the sense of belonging in the Caribbean is conditioned by an always incomplete knowledge of natural and human histories, which necessitates recreating a sense of place in the present." (p. 20) At the end of Part II of *My Garden (Book):*, Kincaid's chapter, "In History," opens and closes, or rather doesn't close, repeats its refrain a second time, in a repeated image of the open wound of history: "an open wound with each breath I take in and expel healing and opening the wound again and again, over and over" (p. 153). This chapter opens onto the complicity between Imperialism and Botany, one that goes to the heart of Kincaid's crises and questioning as a gardener and a person. Although the focus of this discussion is Kincaid's account of her garden, her later work *Among Flowers* (2005) also offers a fascinating counterpoint to the excavation of gardening in its account of her seed hunting travels, in that she undertakes a walking adventure that places her at least alongside, if not retracing, the steps of the explorers and botanists she takes on in *My Garden (Book):*.

As Kincaid reflects on how she is positioned by the account of Christopher Columbus's encounter with and naming of Antigua, she comments that Columbus names the island after a church, and 'empties the land' of the people he finds there; "it is when the land is completely empty that I and the people who look like me begin to make an appearance, the food I eat begins to make an appearance, the trees I will see each day come from far away and begin to make an appearance;..." (1999, p.159).

Kincaid is interested in the provenance of "nature," its history. It is here perhaps that Kincaid's text might engage with and offer nuance to widely deployed concepts—Anthropocene and agrilogistics, both of which have produced numerous qualifications and interventions in current ecocritical discussions. One particularly useful intervention is Donna Haraway's (2015) account of the formulation of the term Plantationocene, as a collectively generated name for the devastating transformations of diverse kinds of human-tended farms, pastures and forests into extractive and enclosed plantations relying on enslaved labour and other forms of exploited, alienated and usually spatially transported unfree workers. "Moving material semiotic generativity around the world for capital accumulation and profit—the rapid displacement and reformulation of germ plasm, genomes, cuttings and all other names and forms of part organism and of deracinated plants, animals and people—is one defining operation of the Plantationocene, Capitalocene, Anthropocene taken together" (2015, p. 162). Her proposal of the Chthulucene seeks to address the ways in which she argues "no species acts alone, assemblages of organic species and abiotic acts make history—the evolutionary kind and other kinds too". (159) Haraway's 'making kin' with human and non-human is made differently by Kincaid as she thinks through her own relation to extractive plantation cultures.

> I do not know any of the plants in the place I am from (Antigua). … The ignorance of the botany of the place I am from (and am of) really only reflects the fact that when I lived there, I was of the conquered class and living in a conquered place; a principle of this condition is that nothing about you is of any interest unless the conqueror deems it so. (1999, pp. 119-120)

Kincaid signals the haunting of the garden by the words that overwrite the plants she is tending to as she recounts the ways in which the history of plant naming went hand in glove with the Imperialist project. Kincaid insists on demystifying the Linnaean taxonomy of plant names as neutral or universal, asserting that Linnaeus too has a history embedded in the Imperialist project. Kincaid explains that Linnaeus found specimens of plants in George Clifford's greenhouse and invented a system of naming, that even she is forced to use:

> The invention of this system has been a good thing. Its narrative would begin in this way: In the beginning, the vegetable kingdom was chaos, people everywhere called the same things by a name that made sense to them, not by a name arrived at by an objective standard. But who has an interest in an objective standard? Who needs one? It makes me ask again, What to call the thing that happened to me and all who look like me? Should I call it history? And if so, what should history mean to someone who looks like me? Should it be an idea; should it be an open wound, each breath I take in and expel healing and opening the wound again, over

> and over, or is it a long moment that begins anew each
> day since 1492? (p. 166)

She comments:

> In almost every account of an event that has taken place
> sometime in the last five hundred years there is always a
> moment when I feel like placing an asterisk somewhere
> in its text and at the end of the official story making
> my own addition. This chapter in the history of botany
> is such a moment. (p. 165)

Kincaid deploys the asterisk as a way of identifying the lacunae, the supressed, occluded histories buried in this botanical landscape. Kincaid's unburying of plant histories, serves as a reminder of Graham Huggan and Helen Tiffin's (2011) argument that "historicization has been a primary tool of postcolonial studies—in order to engage with a historical model of ecology and epistemology of space and time, entering what Wilson Harris suggests is 'a profound dialogue with the landscape'" (p. 75). The Linnaean system, as Mary Louise Pratt comments in *Imperial Eyes: Travel Writing and Transculturation,* "epitomised the transnational aspirations of European science ... Linnaeus deliberately revived Latin for his nomenclature precisely because it was nobody's global language. The fact that he was from Sweden, a relatively minor player in global economic and imperial competition, undoubtedly increased continent wide receptivity to his system" (p. 19). Pratt argues that Linnaeus and his assistants set in motion a project to be realised in the world in the most concrete terms possible: 'a secular global labour,' a totalising classificatory schema that she argues demonstrated a planetary consciousness. It was one, however, that saw the link between naming and owning, between the concrete exploration and classification of plants with geographical and ideological power and appropriation.

As Kincaid's text moves between the autobiographical, local, historical and the global, none of these categories is stable, and one is constantly found imbricated in the other. As Jana Evans Braziel (2009) notes, Kincaid's work is marked by "the entanglement of autobiography with history" (p. 3). It is precisely this spectral presence of Linnaeus that makes Kincaid's book insist on a kind of uncanny world dwelling that thinks the role of writing about plants as vital to a revisiting and remobilisation of the open wound of this history. Looking at nature Kincaid sees culture, and the traumatic histories that mark her own diasporic routes:

> What did the botanical life of Antigua consist of at the time another famous adventurer (Christopher Columbus) first saw it? To see a garden in Antigua will not supply a clue. The bougainvillea (named for another restless European, the sea adventurer Louis de Bougainville, the first Frenchman to cross the Pacific) is native to tropical South America; the plumbago is from southern Africa; the croton from Malaysia; the hibiscus is from Asia (unfringed petal) and East Africa (fringed petal); the allamanda is from Brazil; the poinsettia (named for an American ambassador Joseph Poinsett) is from Mexico; the bird of paradise is from southern Africa; the Bermuda lily is from Japan; ... The breadfruit is from the East Indies. This food, the bread fruit, has been the cause of more disagreement between parents and their children than anything I can think of. No West Indian that I know has ever liked it. It was sent to the West Indies by Joseph Banks, the English naturalist and world traveller, and the founder of Kew Gardens, which was then a clearing house for all the plants stolen from the various parts of the world these people had been .... (p. 135)

Kincaid's uncanny outlining of unnatural nature shares Natasha Tinsley's (2005) observations on Caribbean nature, when she asks "What is natural to the Caribbean? 'Nature' itself is not" (p. 169).

Nestling amongst the list of plant species introduced to Antigua is the detested breadfruit. In Elizabeth DeLoughrey's (2008) seminal account of the cultural and political implications of the movement of breadfruit to the Caribbean from Tahiti by the British in the eighteenth century, she outlines the ways in which the transportation of breadfruit trees served to produce colonial discourses of benevolence towards slaves, as providing much needed nourishment, at a time when antislavery sentiment was increasing, such that the breadfruit was deployed as a tool to sustain a brutal slave economy in the name of a "natural and sustaining food" from Tahiti. "The provision of breadfruit for the slaves was an attempt to displace a growing abolitionist revolution with a scientific one derived from the new knowledges of tropical botany" (p. 1). As DeLoughrey notes, the diaspora of plants has been obscured in studies of globalisation despite the fact that their multiple uses have been crucial to the processes of modernity and its colonial projects. For Kincaid, this unnatural nature, that stories the vast scale of colonial expropriation and distribution, its theft and also its crimes, is written into the landscape by the flourishing of the breadfruit, which materially signals to and mirrors the violent uprooting and exploiting of people. She comments in *My Garden (Book):* (1999):

> And yet the people on Antigua have a relationship to agriculture that cannot please them at all. Their very presence on this island hundreds of years ago has to do with this thing, agriculture. When they (we) were brought to this island from Africa a few hundred years ago, it was not for their pottery-making skills or for their way with a loom; it was for the free labor they could provide in the fields. ... It seems clear to me, then, that a group of people who have had such a horrible historical association with growing things would try to make any relationship to it dignified (agriculture) and useful. (pp. 139-140)

Although Kincaid addresses the breadfruit as a loathed legacy of slavery, she has a more extended contemplation of the significance of another plant connected to plantation labour and resource extraction as a site where other subaltern stories can emerge. In the chapter "The Glasshouse," she recounts her own memories of visiting the Botanical Gardens in Antigua, where she meets foreign plants that are symbols of imperialist botanical mastery, displaying the ease with which transporters such as Joseph Banks could move plants around from one tropical region to another, and the complicity of botany with extractive colonial practices. It is here that she recounts her relationship with the rubber tree, which occupies only a relatively short but nonetheless vital childhood memory in the text (pp. 145-148). This focused memory from her time growing up in Antigua, rather like the asterisk she offers to history, offers a point of entry to a revisiting and reclaiming of unacknowledged and actively denied histories of the plantation as multiple forms of exploitation and considering how to live in the 'wake' of ecological, social and psychic plantation devastation. It offers a route to comprehending and making meaning in the present. In the glasshouse and under the rubber tree, Kincaid shows how the tree itself acts as a signpost for a globalised present. It is here that her father passes on the story of his own life, experienced as a kind of haunting under a tree. The tree chosen by the father is silent witness to the instrumentalization of both indigenous and transported populations and flora and fauna globally, signalling an uncanny worlding in the present in the Botanic Garden.

> The rubber tree from Malaysia (or somewhere) is memorable because in the year my father and I were sick at the same time (he with heart disease, I with hookworms), we would go and sit under this tree after we ate our lunch, and under this tree he would tell me about his parents, who had abandoned him and gone off to build the Panama Canal (though of course he disguised the brutality of this). (p. 120)

Kincaid's account is somewhat less "metaphorical" than that of Benítez-Rojo who famously commented, "Antilleans … tend to roam the entire world in search of the centres of the Caribbeanness, constituting one of our century's most notable migratory flows. The Antillean's insularity does not compel them toward isolation, but on the contrary, toward travel toward exploration toward the search for fluvial and marine routes. One needn't forget that it was men from the Antilles who constructed the Panama Canal" (1992, p. 25). It is under the rubber tree that Kincaid's father speaks of his own family's dispersal to Panama, to work on the Panama Canal. His individual story passed on to her under the sign of transplantation, a rubber tree, signifies the post-emancipation diaspora that produces a huge trans-Caribbean migration, a demographic tidal wave, the largest in Caribbean history leading to the establishment of Afro-Antillean Panamanians who settled in Panama. The transplanted tree in the Glasshouse becomes a ritualised place for Kincaid and her father as they set out together every afternoon during their convalescence from different illnesses: "It was in the shade of the distorted branches of the rubber tree (though this distortion is perfectly natural to the rubber tree) in the botanical garden of St. John's, Antigua, a garden that was the creation of the most ambivalent of people, that I came to know important things, though I came to understand them only long after" (p. 147). It is under the tree that the father can speak of the devastation of his own family, the fate of his ancestors at the hands of Imperialism and where Kincaid experiences the objectification of her father: "It is possible that, in a way, a very human way, my father, when sitting under a rubber tree in the botanical garden, was in the presence, the atmosphere, the shrine of Possession, and that he himself was an object, a mere thing within it" (p. 148).

Reflecting on this moment Kincaid has to perform a kind of thinking and remembering of self that echoes what Christina Sharpe (2016) calls "wake work," a way of reflecting that "avails us particular ways of re/seeing, re/inhabiting, and re/imagining the world." (p. 22) It is necessary I would argue, to read the significance of her father's story in the glasshouse that Kincaid feels, as a sudden and uncanny worlding, a moment that produces an apprehension of the gothic nature of the globalised landscape of Antigua. The rubber tree, itself also transplanted, haunts. It signals for Kincaid, the "people of the mysterious Far East," who "like the people native to everywhere, were workers; that is, they worked in the fields where they cultivated the plants native to their place or the plants that had been made native to their place" (p. 145). Kincaid's belated epiphany (she reflects back on this event and recognises its significance as an adult), under the rubber tree, attempts to signal the effects of multiple violence on those ideologically "distant" geographical locations, where drastic degradation and aggressive resource extraction happen but evade visibility and hence admissions of responsibility. Such an experience of structural myopia is connected to an inability to render, imagine or connect the often invisible structures of global exchange and economy as they impact on specific places. The ecogothic moment of the text insists on linking the plants of one's own garden, grown and tended lovingly, to the longer history of colonial resource extraction and plantation cultures, and the socio-ecological crises that result from this.

Kincaid's uncanny experience under the rubber tree with her father is one of recognition of the interlinked and enmeshed fates of multiple species whose fates and histories cannot be comprehended in isolation. The transplanted tree, that is displayed as a trophy of plantation culture's ability to move peoples and ecologies, speaks, as the father recounts his own multiple dislocations, of the legacies of different moments of forced migrations, of false liberations and continued movements across and between Caribbean locations. If the Anthropocene is to come into view, it is at this moment, at the edges of the child's vision, where the ghosts of the individual life, of the personal story suddenly open into the history of the world itself.

References

Benítez-Rojo, A. (1992). *The Repeating Island: The Caribbean and the Postmodern Perspective.* (J.E. Maraniss,Trans.) Durham, NC and London: Duke University Press. (Original work published 1989)

Braziel, J. E. (2009). *Caribbean Genesis: Jamaica Kincaid and the Writing of New Worlds.* Albany, NY: SUNY Press.

DeLoughrey, E. (2008). Globalizing the Routes of Breadfruit and Other Bounties. *Journal of Colonialism and Colonial History,* 8 (3). Retrieved March 18, 2019, from Project MUSE database

DeLoughrey, E. M., Gosson, R. K. and Handley, G. B. (Eds.) (2005). *Caribbean Literature and the Environment.* Charlottesville, VA and London: University of Virginia Press.

Edwards, J. D. and Vasconcelos, S. G. T. (Eds.) (2016). *Tropical Gothic in Literature and Culture: The Americas.* New York, NY: Routledge.

Haraway, D. (2015). Anthropocene, Capitalocene, Plantationocene, Chthulucene: Making Kin. *Environmental Humanities, 6* (1) 159-165.

Harris, W. (1962). *The Whole Armour and the Secret Ladder.* London: Faber.

Huggan, G. & Tiffin, H. (2011). *Postcolonial Ecocriticism: Literature, Animals, Environment.* New York, NY: Routledge.

Kincaid, J. (1999). *My Garden (Book):*, New York, NY: Farrar, Straus, Giroux.

Kincaid, J. (2005). *Among Flowers: A Walk in the Himalaya*. Washington, DC: National Geographic.

Marder, M. and P. Vieira. (2013). Writing Phytophilia: Philosophers and Poets as Lovers of Plants. *Frame, 26*(2), 37-53.

Marder, M. (2013). *The Philosopher's Plant: An Intellectual Herbarium*. New York, NY: Columbia University Press.

Moore, J. W. (2015). *Capitalism in the Web of Life: Ecology and the Accumulation of Capital*. London and Brooklyn, New York, NY: Verso.

Morton, T. (2016). *Dark Ecology: For a Logic of Future Co-existence*. New York, NY: Columbia University Press.

Pratt, M. L. (1992). *Imperial Eyes: Travel Writing and Transculturation*. New York, NY and London: Routledge.

Sharpe, C. (2016). *In the Wake: On Blackness and Being*. Durham, NC: Duke University Press.

Tinsley, N. (2005). "Rosebud is my mama, stanfaste is my papa": Hybrid Landscapes and Sexualities in Surinamese Oral Literature. In E. M. DeLoughrey, R. K. Gosson & G. B. Handley (Eds.), *Caribbean Literature and the Environment* (pp.169-181). Charlottesville, VA and London: University of Virginia Press.

Wilson, R. (2007). Worlding as Future Tactic. In R. Wilson and C. Leigh Connery (Eds.), *The Worlding Project: Doing Cultural Studies in the Era of Globalisation* (pp. 209-223). Berkeley, CA: North Atlantic Books, New Pacific Press.

EIGHT

REJETER LA GREFFE: FILIATIONS COURT-CIRCUITÉES ET BIOGRAPHIQUE RÉINVENTÉ DANS *THE AUTOBIOGRAPHY OF MY MOTHER*

Natacha d'Orlando
Université Paris 8 Vincennes Saint Denis

Contact: Natacha d'Orlando, Université Paris 8 Vincennes Saint Denis
natachadorlando@gmail.com
To cite this article:
[Natacha d'Orlando. "Rejeter la greffe : Filiations court-circuitées et biographique réinventé dans *The Autobiography of My Mother*." *Wagadu: A Journal of Transnational Women's and Gender Studies,* Summer 2018, vol. 19, pp. 91-105]

Abstract

Le rejet de la maternité par l'avortement permet à Xuela de refuser la « greffe » d'un corps étranger dans le sien afin de déranger l'ordre colonial. Sabotant la lignée masculine Xuela refuse d'être une terre fécondable pour autrui. Par ailleurs, Kincaid efface le récit de sa naissance et fait naître sa mère comme personnage.

Publié en 1996, *The Autobiography of My Mother* prolonge les thématiques abordées dans *Lucy* et *Annie John,* tout en faisant un double pas de côté concernant le motif de la maternité. Si la mère reste un spectre obsédant pour Xuela, la narratrice et protagoniste principale de l'œuvre, ce n'est plus en tant que présence étouffante mais comme une absence, dont la mort laisse un vide abyssal et impossible à combler (Brancato, 2005). Par ailleurs, la maternité n'y est pas uniquement envisagée par l'enfant racontant son rapport à la mère, elle est aussi remise en question par la jeune femme qui risque de devenir mère à son tour. Dans les deux cas, l'expérience maternelle se construit sur la négation, l'héroïne orpheline mettant un terme à chacune de ses grossesses, celle qui n'a derrière elle qu'un vide insondable (« at my back was always a bleak, black wind », Kincaid, 1996, p. 3) choisissant de prolonger cet abîme à travers les avortons qu'elle voue au précipice (« In their day of life, I would walk them to the edge of a precipice », p. 97). Xuela n'est pas la seule protagoniste à envisager ou à réaliser une interruption de grossesse, et l'avortement s'inscrit dans deux pôles thématiques centraux de l'œuvre de Kincaid : l'usage des plantes et le rapport à la maternité. Les breuvages emménagogues ou abortifs occupent un domaine féminin du savoir, un élément du « travail domestique » (Kincaid, 2000, p. 90) fondé sur un ensemble de pratiques transmises de mère en fille. Dans *Lucy,* la narratrice se rappelle ainsi les enseignements reçus pendant l'enfance :

> Without telling me exactly how I might miss a menstrual
> cycle, my mother had shown me which herbs to pick
> and boil, and what time of day to drink the potion
> they produced, to bring on a reluctant period. She had

> presented the whole idea to me as a way to strengthen
> the womb, but underneath we both knew that a weak
> womb was not the cause of a missed period. (p. 69)

L'introduction de Lucy à la sexualité se fonde sur un jeu de dupe féminin entre une mère qui, sans nommer ni décrire la sexualité, apprend à sa fille à se défaire d'une grossesse indésirable, et une fille qui formule silencieusement les non-dits de sa génitrice (« She knew that I knew », p. 70). De la même manière, dans *At the Bottom of the River*, l'une des recommandations de la mère et narratrice de « Girl », soucieuse d'empêcher sa fille de devenir une « catin », concerne paradoxalement la manière de préparer un breuvage abortif : « this is how to make a good medicine to throw away a child before it even becomes a child » (1983, p. 5). La discussion fille / mère qui accompagne les premières règles et sanctionne le passage à l'âge adulte prend la forme d'une formation accélérée en plantes emménagogues et passe par la transmission matrilinéaire d'une connaissance et d'une pratique de santé non médicalisée. Contrairement à d'autres représentations littéraires de l'avortement, celle de Paule Marshall dans *Daughters* ou d'Alice Walker dans *Meridian,* où la scène abortive prend place dans un cadre hospitalier, professionnel et majoritairement masculin, l'acte repose toujours chez Kincaid sur les préceptes d'une pharmacopée afro-caribéenne féminine, ensemble des savoirs et pratiques d'héroïnes qui cultivent, récoltent et préparent elles-mêmes les moyens d'agir sur leur corps. Dans une nature colonisée et pillée par les botanistes européens (Kincaid, 2000; Schiebinger, 2004), ces avortements marquent la survie d'un matrimoine scientifique caribéen, fondé sur un savoir empirique des corps et des plantes.

En outre, les scènes d'avortements s'inscrivent dans le tableau que dresse Kincaid des maternités conflictuelles, en particulier lorsqu'elles sont envisagées par un personnage qui se croit ou se sait né de l'échec des avortements de sa mère. Dans *Mr. Potter,* la narratrice revient ainsi sur une confidence faite par sa mère qui lui avoua, quelques années plus tôt, avoir tenté de mettre un terme à sa grossesse pendant qu'elle l'attendait

: « And when my mother tried to force her menstruation unnaturally for the fifth time, she failed and that failure was because of me, I could not be expelled from my mother's womb at her own will » (p. 136). De la même manière, dans *My Brother,* Devon, qui semble avoir lu les passages de *Lucy* où la mère tente d'interrompre sa dernière grossesse, lui demande : « ("Ah me de trow'way pickney") (Am I an unwanted child?) » (p. 174).

The Autobiography of My Mother est l'œuvre dans laquelle l'avortement occupe la place la plus grande, à la fois par la récurrence des scènes et discours s'y rapportant et du fait de l'importance de ces épisodes dans la construction du personnage principal. Quatre spécificités distinguent les avortements de Xuela de ceux évoqués dans *Lucy, My Brother, Mr. Potter* ou *My Garden (Book):* : pour la première fois, l'avortement n'est pas uniquement mentionné, envisagé ou imaginé, il est vécu et décrit à la première personne, s'inscrivant ainsi dans le réseau des expériences corporelles qui jalonnent le récit de Xuela et cimentent sa conscience subjective. Ensuite, le geste ne relève pas d'un choix ponctuel et circonstanciel, mais d'un refus global et systématique, rendu explicite par la narratrice qui déclare : « I had never had a mother, I had just recently refused to become one, and I knew then that this refusal would be complete » (p. 97). Xuela évoque ici une autre particularité du refus de maternité dans son récit : le lien entre cette décision et la mort de sa mère qui influence à la fois son rapport à la filiation et son accès aux savoirs abortifs, la privant du réseau matrilinéaire de transmission dont pouvait profiter Lucy. Enfin, les avortements sont intégrés à une œuvre intitulée *The Autobiography of My Mother* et mettent en question le fondement biographique du récit d'une mère caractérisée précisément par son refus de devenir mère. Tandis que, dans *Annie John* et *Lucy,* Kincaid remontait en arrière pour mettre en fiction ses années d'enfance, elle sonde ici les décennies qui précèdent sa naissance et remonte jusqu'au spectre à la fois obsédant et angoissant de l'avortement maternel.

C'est en nous fondant sur ces spécificités que nous aborderons le motif abortif dans *The Autobiography of My Mother*, envisagé comme le moyen de résister aux greffes que tentent de lui imposer Monsieur et Madame LaBatte, les premiers employeurs de Xuela, son père ou son amant Roland, qui tentent d'implanter dans sa matrice un fruit étranger qu'ils sont seuls voués à récolter. Xuela rejette la greffe, à la fois de manière consciente et volontaire, refusant de porter le fruit d'une hybridation non-consentie, et de manière instinctive, portée par la réaction intuitive d'un sujet que toute sa condition individuelle, collective et historique rend incapable de devenir mère. L'avortement est donc à la fois un symptôme et un perturbateur, un indice de la condition individuelle et historique de Xuela et, dans le même temps, un acte de « résistance gynécologique » (Beckles, 1989) contre l'aliénation d'un corps sur lequel Xuela fonde toute son identité. En ce sens, il permet de représenter à la fois un corps décolonisé, court-circuitant les logiques de son exploitation, et un corps sur-colonisé, témoignant de la permanence d'un schéma colonial antagoniste des valeurs et fonctions associées à la maternité.

Greffe de corps : fécondation, possession, colonisation ; La machine (re)productive : ventre-ressources

Dans la Dominique coloniale qu'habite Xuela, la maternité reste un objet politique sur lequel repose une partie de la survie de l'Empire. Colonisation et maternité se trouvent donc indéfectiblement liées dans leurs principes, leurs valeurs et leurs réalisations. Cette association s'ancre dans le contexte historique caribéen, prenant source dans le système plantationnaire où les ventres étaient exploités pour produire des esclaves et la reproduction subordonnée aux logiques d'accumulation du capital, ainsi que le décrit Hazel Carby dans le contexte états-unien : « Black women gave birth to property and, directly, to capital itself in the form of slaves » (Carby, 1987, p. 24). La maternité blanche a aussi occupé les politiques et discours coloniaux, à la fois littéralement, lorsque les mères britanniques étaient encouragées à soutenir l'expansion de l'Empire en mettant au monde et en élevant ses futurs agents (Davin, 1978; Perry,

1991), et métaphoriquement, la métropole coloniale étant alors désignée comme la mère-patrie que doivent honorer ses enfants colonisés, à l'image de cette maxime inventée par l'institutrice Mrs. Hinds dans *Crick Crack Monkey* : « Not an eyelid must bat not a finger must twitch when we honour the Mother Country » (Hodge, 1970, p. 26).

La maternité est aussi une question coloniale pour Xuela, qui associe parenté et expansion coloniale comme deux expressions d'un même désir de pouvoir. Cette association s'annonce dans l'épisode des trois tortues dont Xuela tombe amoureuse pendant son enfance et qu'elle parque dans un endroit clos afin d'assurer leur subsistance tout en les rendant entièrement dépendantes ; elle les soigne et les nourrit jusqu'à ce que, vexée de les voir rentrer leur tête dans leur carapace, elle bouche le trou qui leur permettait de survivre, les oublie et les laisse mourir (pp. 11-12). Cette scène se déploie sur plusieurs niveaux de sens : elle est à la fois une miniature de l'existence de Xuela (Brancato, 2005), une représentation de l'amour maternel omnipotent et destructeur où la mère qui nourrit est aussi celle qui punit et une réplique de la conquête et de la colonisation. Dans cette dernière lecture, les tortues figurent les îles caribéennes victimes, elles aussi, d'un désir destructeur de posséder et de soumettre. Réapparaît ici la métaphore employée par Derek Walcott dans « The Star-Apple Kingdom » où il représente l'archipel comme un ensemble de tortues de tailles et d'espèces différentes : « Islands that coupled as sadly as turtles / engendering islets, as the turtle of Cuba / mounting Jamaica engendered the Caymans, as, behind / the hammerhead turtle of Haiti-San Domingo / trailed the little turtles from Tortuga to Tobago » (Walcott, 1979, p. 104). C'est le même désir de maternité / colonisation qui conduit tour à tour Lise LaBatte à vouloir épouser Monsieur LaBatte, à souhaiter devenir mère, à espérer trouver en sa jeune domestique une fille de substitution, et, finalement, à envisager de lui faire porter l'enfant qu'elle ne peut pas concevoir. Dans cette quête de possession, Lise cherche à la fois à greffer ces identités à la sienne, à exister grâce à l'époux ou l'enfant, et à se greffer sur eux dans une union organique indéfectible:

> [Lise] wanted only to have [Monsieur LaBatte]; he would
> not be had, he would not be contained. To want what you
> will never have and to know too late that you will never
> have it is a life overwhelmed with sadness. She wanted a
> child, but her womb was like a sieve; it would not contain
> a child, it would not contain anything now (p. 76).

A la source du désir maternel de Lise se trouve une volonté de contenir (« contain ») l'autre dans un sens à la fois spatial et affectif, de le porter comme une mère et de le maîtriser comme un maître. Confrontée à sa stérilité biologique, Lise est forcée de transférer ce désir sur l'enfant que pourrait porter Xuela, plaçant ses espérances dans une grossesse qu'elle organise en silence jusqu'à ce que Xuela comprenne finalement la teneur de son projet secret : « She wanted something again from me, she wanted a child I might have » (p. 77). Jamais Xuela n'est vouée à devenir la mère de l'enfant à naître, aussi est-ce Lise qui lui révèle cette grossesse (« She said I was "with child" », p. 81), prenant soin de ne pas utiliser l'adjectif « enceinte » pour insister sur le seul rapport contenant/ contenu qui lie Xuela et cet enfant qu'elle considère comme le sien. A la disparition du fœtus, c'est encore Lise seule qui porte le deuil : « She was in mourning. Her eyes were black and shiny with tears » (p. 94). Ainsi, lors de son premier avortement, Xuela refuse non pas de devenir mère mais de devenir une génitrice pour les LaBatte, une terre passive, à ensemencer et dont les fruits lui seraient enlevés pour satisfaire les désirs de possession d'une autre. En avortant de cet enfant-greffon, Xuela met en échec ce schéma colonial fondé sur l'externalisation de la (re)production et s'extrait de cette exploitation organisée de sa matrice.

« I refused to belong to a race, I refused to accept a nation » : Saboter les lignées

La première grossesse de Xuela ne s'inscrit pas uniquement dans le projet élaboré par Lise, elle répond aussi au dessein d'un père qui semble avoir lui-même offert le corps de sa fille au couple des LaBatte, organisant sa descendance selon ses propres plans et attentes. Aussi les avortements prennent-ils également sens à l'échelle familiale et permettent à Xuela de saboter une lignée paternelle dont elle se sait irrémédiablement exclue. Deux branches généalogiques distinctes émergent en effet dans *The Autobiography of My Mother* : d'une part, une branche masculine et euro-descendante, dans laquelle les fils héritent de leur père un nom, un destin et une apparence, de l'autre, une branche féminine, caribéenne ou afro-descendante, constituée d'aïeules sans prénom, sans histoire et sans visage. D'un côté, la dynastie des John et des Alfred, de l'autre la lignée décimée des aînées anonymes, à la fois du côté maternel, Xuela ne connaît ni sa mère ni la grand-mère qui a abandonné sa fille à la naissance, et du côté paternel, Mary, la grand-mère africaine, n'ayant laissé presque aucune trace dans la mémoire d'un fils qui ne dispose même pas d'une photo pour se remémorer son visage (« I do not know if his mother was beautiful; there was no picture of her and my father never spoke of her in that way », p. 182). Inconnus ou oubliés, les personnages féminins ne prennent pas place dans le réseau intergénérationnel de transmission qu'est la lignée, n'ayant aucun bien ni richesse dont pourraient hériter leurs fil-le-s sinon un legs de défaite et de dépossession : les traits caraïbes de Xuela (p. 15), le prénom inscrit sur la couverture qui enveloppait sa mère quand elle fut abandonnée (p. 80) ou la lampe qui éclaire son premier rapport sexuel avec Philip (p. 150).

Les personnages masculins, au contraire, transmettent à leurs enfants une partie de ce qu'ils sont, possèdent et projettent. Comme dans *Mr. Potter* les figures paternelles sont représentées comme des fécondateurs en série, essaimant derrière eux des fil-le-s illégitimes qui leur permettent, à la manière d'un colonisateur, de modeler le paysage à leur image et de laisser trace de leur passage. Ainsi John Richardson, l'ancêtre écossais de Xuela, survit dans les mémoires grâce aux enfants à cheveux roux qu'il sème derrière lui et qui peuplent les îles qu'il a habitées, semblables à des vestiges architecturaux d'une civilisation coloniale (p. 182). Même les personnages les plus dépossédés saisissent cette paternité en série comme le seul mode de conquête auquel ils sont susceptibles d'avoir accès, à l'image de Roland qui jauge sa réussite au nombre des amantes qu'il a rendues mères, substituant aux noms des pays conquis ceux des enfants conçus : « His life was reduced to a list of names that were not countries, and to the number of times he brought the monthly flow of blood to a halt » (p. 175). La paternité offre à ces personnages une forme d'immortalité, à la fois par la transmission de leur patrimoine matériel et par la reproduction de soi dans un fils transformé, comme le frère de Xuela, en un double malheureux du père : « [My father] had imagined himself as continuing to live on through the existence of someone else » (p. 110). Prenant exemple sur son propre géniteur, Alfred Richardson rêve d'établir sa petite dynastie familiale (« his own small dynasty of red-haired boys », p. 182) et de greffer sa descendance sur les corps de ses compagnes, dans un geste botanique que souligne Xuela lorsqu'elle présente les avortons comme des fruits dont elle serait la vigne : « I would bear [children] in abundance ; they would hang from me like fruit from a vine » (p. 97). Kincaid reprend ici l'image biblique du raisin, symbole de la reproduction humaine dans des textes où l'épouse est désignée « comme [la] vigne féconde dans l'intérieur de [la] maison » (Psaume, 128:3). Un peu plus loin, le « grape » devient « grapefruit » lorsqu'elle se rappelle sa visite dans les jardins de son père :

> He told me that the grapefruit was natural to the West Indies, that sometime in the seventeenth century it had mutated from the Ugli fruit on the island of Jamaica. He said this in a way that made me think he wanted the grapefruit and himself to be One. (p. 102)

En introduisant Xuela chez les LaBatte, le père rêve de reproduire par l'hybridation cette mutation génétique dont il est à la fois le jardinier et le fruit, plantant, croisant et cultivant sa descendance jusqu'à faire germer des pamplemousses sur ses graines de tangelo. Par là, il cherche aussi à réactiver le schéma d'exploitation qu'il mit en place, enfant, avec la poule offerte par une voisine :

> That chicken became a hen and laid eggs and those eggs were set and became chickens and those chickens laid eggs and so on, an endless cycle interrupted only by

> the sale of some eggs and some chickens, and with the
> farthings, halfpennies, and pennies that they brought in
> exchange and profit. He never ate eggs after that (not all
> the time I knew him); he never ate chickens after that
> (not all the time I knew him), only collecting the bright
> red copper of money and polishing it so that it shone
> and giving it to his mother, who placed it in an old sock
> and kept it in her bosom awake and asleep. (p. 194)

Les femelles sont, pour le père de Xuela, garantes de la production et de la conservation des biens masculins, qu'il s'agisse de la poule couvant ses œufs ou de la mère chargée de garder les pièces de son fils. Dans cet extrait, le rapport entre production et reproduction est renforcé par l'image des pièces de cuivre, équivalent pécuniaire des descendant-e-s aux cheveux cuivrés de John Richardson, et par la cyclicité d'une exploitation vouée à renaître et à se prolonger indéfiniment.

En interrompant ses grossesses et en aidant sa demi-sœur à avorter, Xuela met en échec les rêves dynastiques de son géniteur et proclame son refus d'être la vigne, l'arbre, ou la poule, de transmettre un héritage masculin de conquête et de dépossession. Dans le même temps, elle renoue avec l'héritage des vaincues, des mères caraïbes ou des descendantes d'esclaves, exclues d'une lignée qu'elles participent pourtant à prolonger. Ainsi, au terme de son premier avortement, et après avoir parcouru mentalement son île, elle peut déclarer : « I walked through my inheritance » (p. 89). Mettant en pratique sa devise « I am not a people, I am not a nation » (p. 216), Xuela s'autonomise de toute construction collective généalogique ou nationale, de toute contribution biologique à la "nation" ou à la "race" (Raiskin, 1996, p. 7). Comme une île en recherche d'autonomie, elle assouvit aussi sa pulsion auto-émancipatrice (Snodgrass, 2008), cette obsession autarcique qui la pousse à refuser la structure du foyer quelle que puisse y être sa place (fille, sœur, compagne ou mère), à rejeter toutes les potentielles mères de substitution et à préférer au couple le trio amoureux. Cette quête effrénée d'autonomie la pousse, enfin, à dicter sa loi à un corps qu'elle finit par maîtriser à la seule force de sa volonté, subordonnant son fonctionnement biologique à la règle qu'elle s'est elle-même choisie : « For years and years, each month my body would swell up slightly, mimicking the state of maternity, longing to conceive, mourning my heart's and mind's decision never to bring forth a child » (p. 226). L'avortement est ainsi un geste offensif dans une lutte qui l'oppose tour à tour aux LaBatte, à son père, à Roland ou à son propre corps.

Semences stériles : le destin abortif

Si l'on peut lire les avortements de Xuela comme des gestes de revendication et de résistance, il faut aussi se pencher sur le refus de la maternité dans une perspective historique et collective comme étant la trace d'une incapacité héritée à devenir mère. Dans *The Daughter's Return: African-American and Caribbean Women's Fictions of History* (2000), Caroline Rody se penche sur les rapports mère/fille conflictuels dans les littératures africaines-américaines et caribéennes et propose de les lire comme des métaphores du rapport problématique des héroïnes à l'Histoire (« mother-as-history »). Le refus de maternité signe l'entrée des héroïnes dans une « mauvaise » ou dans une « fausse histoire », il matérialise la présence obsédante d'un passé traumatique qui détruit dans l'œuf toute perspective de futur. Dans *The Autobiography of My Mother*, la systématisation de l'avortement, le rejet instinctif de la greffe révèlent aussi la condition d'une héroïne incapable de devenir mère, non pas sur le plan biologique mais sur le plan affectif.

Grossesse, pathologie, invasion : le parasite fœtal

La stérilité volontaire de Xuela fonctionne en miroir avec l'absence originelle de la mère, paramètre qui conditionne intégralement son rapport à la maternité biologique et affective. Cette maternité lui apparaît d'abord comme un événement anormal et inquiétant, un phénomène rendu étranger par le manque d'une interlocutrice féminine pour le lui expliquer. Jusqu'à sa première grossesse, Xuela parvient à comprendre seule le fonctionnement de son corps, affirmant par exemple, à l'arrivée de ses règles : « I knew immediately that its failure to appear regularly after a certain interval could only mean a great deal of trouble for me » (p. 57). Reliant instinctivement menstruation et maternité, Xuela occupe la fonction maternelle vacante et recrée un enseignement que dans *Lucy* il incombait à la mère de transmettre à sa fille : « And then she said that finding blood in my underpants might be something one day I would get down on my knees and pray for » (Kincaid, 1990, p. 69). Ce rapport de transparence entre Xuela et son corps se brise dès les premiers signes de sa grossesse : « One day I became very sick. I was with child but I did not know it. I had no experience with the symptoms of such a state and so did not immediately know what was happening to me » (p. 81). Née d'une mère morte pendant l'accouchement, Xuela envisage irrémédiablement la grossesse comme un événement pathologique, dangereux et mortel, une maladie féminine à laquelle n'a pas survécu sa propre génitrice. En se découvrant enceinte, elle ne pense ni aux LaBatte, ni à l'enfant qu'elle porte, seulement à l'intense et brutale angoisse de mort qui s'empare d'elle : « I believed that I would die, and perhaps because I no longer had a future I began to want one very much » (p. 82). Déjà, en découvrant le projet de Lise, Xuela s'était imaginée à la fois morte et enceinte, liant instinctivement ces deux expériences fondamentalement inconnues :

> She wanted something again from me, she wanted a child I might have; I did not let her know that I heard that, and this vision she would have, of a child inside me, eventually in her arms, hung in the air like a ghost, something only the special could see. Not for every eye, it was for my eyes, but I would never see it, and it would go away and come back, this ghost of me with a child inside me. I turned my back to it; my ears grew deaf to it; my heart would not beat. (p. 77)

L'image du fantôme dit la dépossession d'un personnage que le projet de Lise exclurait de son propre corps, séparant le « je » de cette image spectrale de lui-même. Elle traduit en même temps l'angoisse de Xuela face à une grossesse qu'elle s'imagine lui être fatale. L'avortement est dès lors dicté par un réflexe de survie, il constitue d'abord un geste thérapeutique voué à provoquer l'expulsion nécessaire et vitale d'un amas de cellules pathologiques.

Xuela avorte pour ne pas connaître le même destin que sa mère morte pendant l'accouchement. Parallèlement, ses avortements la mettent plus que jamais en contact avec cette génitrice inconnue, avec les douleurs de l'enfantement et avec le sang utérin qui la ramène à la scène de sa propre naissance :

> I was wet between my legs; I could smell the wetness; it was blood, fresh and old. The fresh blood smelled like a newly dug-up mineral that had not yet been refined and turned into something worldly, something to which a value could be assigned. The old blood gave off a sweet rotten stink, and this I loved and would breathe in deeply when it came to dominate the other smells in the room; perhaps I only loved it because it was mine. (p. 91)

Avec son odeur de pierre, le sang neuf incarne à la fois l'origine, la matière brute et atemporelle, et la naissance d'un objet tout juste extrait du sol-matrice. Mais par son odeur de pourriture et de dégradation, il évoque aussi la mort, le temps passé et le corps maternel morbide. Dans ces deux sangs, Xuela se lie avec le corps parental retrouvé, enivrée par son parfum comme l'est la jeune Annie John lorsqu'elle colle son nez contre la peau de sa mère afin de prolonger olfactivement l'indistinction originelle de leurs deux corps (p. 22). Les avortements ne sont pas uniquement une expérience de la rupture, ils mettent Xuela au contact de sa mère, de ses aïeul-e-s, et, plus généralement, d'une communauté des vaincus partageant avec les avortons une existence incomplète et anonyme. En les vouant à une souffrance éternelle, à une non-existence dans un monde sans amour, Xuela introduit les avortons dans l'espace qu'elle habite et en fait les membres de la lignée des déshérités qu'ils n'auraient que partiellement habitée s'ils étaient venus au monde. De la même manière que son frère ne le devient qu'au moment de sa mort (« In death he became my brother », p. 110), et sa sœur qu'après son avortement (p. 114), les avortons de Xuela ne peuvent être ses enfants qu'à condition de toujours appartenir, comme elle, au clan des vaincus et de partager son existence de souffrance et de désespoir. La seule parenté que peut reconnaître Xuela est celle de la défaite, de la dépossession et de l'anonymat.

L'impossible maternité affective

Dès ses premières règles, Xuela sait qu'elle n'aura jamais la capacité émotionnelle de devenir mère : « Perhaps I knew then that the child in me would never be stilled enough to allow me to have a child on my own » (p. 57). Enceinte, elle doit composer avec deux enfants en elle : celui qu'elle a intériorisé faute de l'avoir jamais incarné et celui qui s'est logé dans sa matrice, deux présences concurrentes qui s'excluent mutuellement. L'enfant à naître met en péril la stratégie de survie narcissique élaborée par Xuela, qui s'abîme dans l'amour-propre et l'observation autarcique de soi pour pallier l'absence d'amour maternel : « No one observed and beheld me, I observed and beheld myself; the invisible current went out and it came back to me » (p. 56). Au sein de ce couple parental reconstitué où Xuela est à la fois la mère et l'enfant, l'observante et l'observée, le fœtus apparaît comme un perturbateur et un concurrent, une présence indésirable qu'elle élimine pour ne pas avoir à transformer son amour propre en amour maternel. Cette rivalité jalouse s'exprime dans la pulsion violente dirigée contre des avortons qu'elle s'imagine dévorer, fracturant leur squelette et ornant leur cadavre de plaies purulentes dans une longue tirade susceptible d'être lue comme l'expression de la haine jalouse d'un enfant face aux rivaux qu'il tente d'éliminer et sur qui il exerce sa toute-puissance divine et meurtrière (pp. 96-98). La cruauté de la narratrice peut aussi être mise en rapport avec le sentiment de jalousie exprimé par d'autres personnages de Kincaid à la naissance de leurs jeunes frères (1990, p. 129).

Acte de destruction et d'extermination, l'avortement de Xuela constitue aussi une forme d'auto-génération et d'accouchement de soi, une expérience sanglante et si douloureuse qu'elle la considère comme une définition même de la douleur (« it was as if it defined pain itself », p. 82), utilisant là une expression qui réapparaît, dans *Mr. Potter* pour décrire la naissance du père de la narratrice («... a definition of pain itself... », p. 66). Xuela accouche d'elle-même en expulsant le fœtus indésirable, déclarant au terme de ces quatre jours de souffrance être devenue une nouvelle personne (« I was a new person then . . . I had carried my own life in my own hands », p. 83) avant de revenir au monde sous les traits d'un ermite à la fois femme et homme, doté d'une apparence et d'une identité nouvelle. L'avortement lui permet donc de survivre et de renaître, de ne pas se laisser vaincre par un enfant qui l'expose à la disparition, à la fois sur le plan physique et sur le plan affectif. Préférant l'auto-génération à la maternité, Xuela refuse de détruire la scène narcissique sur laquelle elle est à la fois la mère et l'enfant et exhibe sa propre incapacité à devenir mère sans avoir connu la sienne et à alimenter un désir maternel qui lui est entièrement étranger.

Cette incapacité est également le reflet d'une constitution collective modelée par l'Histoire et incompatible avec les valeurs de la filiation, de la famille, voire de la communauté. Xuela envisage l'amour comme un sentiment inconnu, étranger aux vaincus qui sont dépossédés de tout : « all that is unreal, all that is not human, all that is without love, all that is without mercy » (p. 37). Partant, aucune forme d'amour ou d'affection ne peut s'établir entre mère (biologique ou de substitution) et enfant, ainsi que l'observe Xuela chez Ma Eunice :

> Ma Eunice was not unkind: she treated me just the way she treated her own children—but this is not to say she was kind to her own children. In a place like this, brutality is the only real inheritance and cruelty is sometimes the only thing freely given. (p. 5)

A cause de sa condition sociale et historique, Ma Eunice ne peut devenir la mère tendre, douce et aimante qui fonde l'idéal de la maternité blanche mythifiée et essentialisée, (Greenfield & Barash, 1999 ; Welter, 1966), elle se trouve contrainte à incarner la « mauvaise mère » brutale, cruelle et maltraitante. Représentant l'amour maternel comme un privilège dont l'Histoire a privé les vaincus, Kincaid met en scène le lien indéfectible entre les conceptions de la maternité et les logiques de race, de classe et de genre qui les informent et les modifient (Collins, 1994). Aucune des relations mère/enfant dépeintes dans *The Autobiography of My Mother* ne semble ainsi plus enviable que la condition d'orpheline de Xuela, les mères étant toujours des inconnues pour leurs fils et des ennemies pour leurs filles. Haïssant naturellement ce qui leur ressemble, rejetant la fonction mimétique essentielle à tout système familial (Spartacus, 2014), elles repoussent l'image dupliquée d'elles-mêmes que leur présente leur fille, à l'image de l'épouse du père de Xuela qui « préférait son fils parce qu'il n'était pas comme elle » :

> That she did not think very much of the person who was most like her, a daughter, a female, was so normal that it would have been noticed only if it had been otherwise: to people like us, despising anything that was most like ourselves was almost a law of nature. (p. 52)

Pour des mères éduquées à détester tout ce qui constitue leur identité, les filles ne sont que des doubles repoussants et naturellement haïssables, trop ressemblants pour qu'elles ne les méprisent pas. Ce legs de brutalité et de haine de soi contribue aussi au refus de maternité formulé par Xuela, dont les avortements ne sont pas en ce sens antithétiques de la maternité puisqu'ils reproduisent et accentuent la pulsion de violence observée chez Ma Eunice ou l'épouse de son père. En brisant ces futurs enfants qu'elle se sait incapable d'aimer, Xuela réalise un geste paradoxalement maternel et exhibe le mode de maternité propre aux vaincu-e-s et aux dépossédé-e-s. Cette maternité monstrueuse réapparaît d'ailleurs dans les angoisses infantiles d'autres jeunes narratrices de Kincaid qui décrivent leur mère comme une figure ambivalente et dangereuse. Ainsi, la mère anthropophage incarnée par Xuela (« I would eat them at night, swallowing them whole, all at once », p. 97) rappelle les craintes de Lucy qui, évoquant la grossesse de sa mère, parle de l'époque où elle était dans son « estomac » (« This woman he had children with tried to kill me when I was in my mother's stomach », p. 80) et substitue l'organe de la gestation à celui de la dévoration. Le refus de maternité est, pour Xuela, un symptôme de sa réalité individuelle et historique ainsi qu'un révélateur de la stérilité affective de sujets sans amour, sans histoire, sans lignée.

Auto-générations : stériliser la mère, accoucher (de) la génitrice

Dans *Caribbean Genesis: Jamaica Kincaid and the Writing of New Worlds* (2009), Jana Evans Braziel revient sur le conflit central, dans *The Autobiography of My Mother*, entre l'aspect biographique de l'œuvre, indiqué par le titre et l'image de couverture, et le fait qu'elle soit désignée comme un « roman ». Ce paradoxe est alimenté par les scènes d'avortement qui semblent fermer la possibilité d'une lecture biographique pourtant encouragée par le retour de scènes reprises d'autres récits et qui invitent à lire en Xuela une version légèrement modifiée de la mère d'Annie ou de Lucy, voire une version fictive de la véritable mère de Kincaid. Ainsi, dans *Mr. Potter*, la narratrice crée une miniature du récit de Xuela lorsqu'elle retrace brièvement l'histoire de sa mère, tandis que l'épisode du caillou lancé au visage par un singe rappelle un souvenir d'enfance vécu et raconté par la mère de Lucy. Kincaid semble ainsi livrer, avec *The Autobiography of My Mother,* une fiction partiellement biographique construite à partir des récits de sa mère. Elle brise pourtant ce rapport d'identification en faisant de Xuela un personnage sans descendance, détruisant le lien de filiation qui pourrait la rattacher à ce « je » dont elle ne deviendra jamais la fille. Ce nœud de contradiction permet à Kincaid de redéfinir le rapport de son œuvre avec le réel et le factuel, ainsi qu'elle l'expose à Dwight Garner en 1996 :

It was a deliberate choice. It is somewhat explained in
the book — that the main character is a fertile woman
who decides not to be. And that is drawn from an
observation I've made about my own mother: That all
her children are quite happy to have been born, but
all of us are quite sure she should never have been a
mother. I feel comfortable saying that publicly, I think.
I try not to corner my mother anymore. Because I
have at my disposal a way of articulating things about
her that she can't respond to. But I feel comfortable
saying that the core of the book — and the book is not
autobiographical except in this one way — derives from
the observation that my own mother should not have
had children. (p. 5)

Le seul élément biographique admis par Kincaid est le rapport
problématique de son héroïne à la maternité. Dans une tentative
d'avortement réussie, contre-point positif à l'échec enregistré plus tard
dans *Mr. Potter*, corrigeant les choix de sa génitrice en l'empêchant de
devenir mère, Kincaid réécrit son histoire familiale en s'effaçant du
tableau. Par ce jeu de greffe sur le réel d'éléments antinomiques du réel,
Kincaid construit une autobiographie du non-réalisé, le récit d'une vie
semi-fictive fondée sur ce qui aurait dû être autant que sur ce qui a été,
actualisant ce qui, jusque-là, était resté latent. Elle ancre ainsi son œuvre
dans un espace intermédiaire entre le réel et le fictif, lieu de reprise et
de transformation qui caractérise pour elle la fiction : « The process of
fiction, for me, is using reality and then reinventing reality, which is the
most successful way to do what I do » (Vorda, p. 92).

Le refus de maternité de Xuela fonctionne aussi comme un révélateur
du lien entre fiction et filiation, entre mise en récit et mise au monde.
Par cette œuvre qui se signale comme autobiographique, Kincaid donne
naissance à une mère qu'elle rebaptise et dont elle change la destinée,
faisant d'elle un personnage partiellement autonome de son modèle non-
fictif. Inversant les rôles entre celle qui crée et celle qui est créée, elle

s'affirme comme la génitrice littéraire de cette mère devenue Xuela, ainsi que l'indique l'apparition par étapes de sa photographie, dévoilée de la tête aux hanches au fil du récit, comme le corps d'un nourrisson naissant de la matrice littéraire créée par Kincaid. Cette inversion du rapport parent/enfant réapparaît de manière plus explicite dans *Mr. Potter,* où l'illettrisme du père de la narratrice donne à la fille un ascendant quasi maternel sur son géniteur :

> I still managed to acquire the ability to read and the ability to write and in this way I make Mr. Potter and in this way I unmake Mr. Potter, and apart from the fact that he is now dead, he is unable to affect the portrait of him I am rendering here, the scenes on the bolt of cloth as he appears in them: the central figure. (p. 158)

Pouvoir écrire le père, c'est pouvoir le créer, inverser le rapport de filiation et tenir dans sa main celui qui, de son vivant, refusa d'occuper la fonction parentale. Puisqu'il n'est jamais devenu un père pour sa fille, il devient pour elle un enfant, une créature littéraire qu'il sera incapable de corriger ou de contester. Les récits familiaux de Kincaid et ses intrusions dans le champ biographique indiquent ainsi sa manière de créer un espace concurrent au réel, dans lequel elle bouleverse le rapport hiérarchique parent/enfant. La représentation de l'avortement nous indique ainsi comment Jamaica Kincaid, s'emparant d'un motif-clé des discours et luttes féministes, en fait un objet à la fois intime, politique et littéraire. Plus qu'un sujet de revendication, l'avortement sert à la construction de son personnage principal, à la révélation des mécanismes de pouvoir en jeu dans son récit et à la mise en lumière de son mode d'écriture et de fictionnalisation du réel. Si ces récits peuvent être qualifiés de féministes, c'est seulement de manière indirecte et non-revendicative, comme le témoignage d'une condition, d'une intimité et d'une pensée féminine individuelles, ainsi qu'elle le déclare lors d'un entretien en 1990 : « I wrote that way because that was the way I could write, so it does not feel to me that this is the way women write » (Cudjoe, p. 222).

Références

Barash, C. & Greenfield, S. (Eds.). (1999). *Inventing Maternity: Politics, Science and Literature, 1650-1865*. Lexington, KY: University Press of Kentucky.

Beckles, H. (1989). *Natural Rebels: A Social History of Enslaved Black Women in Barbados*. New Brunswick, NJ: Rutgers University Press.

Brancato, S. (2001). *Mother and Motherland in Jamaica Kincaid*. Frankfurt am Main: Lang.

Braziel, J.E (2009). *Caribbean Genesis: Jamaica Kincaid and the Writing of New Worlds*. Albany, NY: State University of New York Press.

Carby, H. (1987). *Reconstructing Womanhood: The Emergence of the Afro-American Woman Novelist*. Oxford: Oxford University Press.

Collins, P. (1994). Shifting the Center: Race, Class, and Feminist Theorizing about Motherhood. In E. Glenn, G. Chang, L. Forcey (Eds.), *Mothering: Ideology, Experience, and Agency* (pp. 45-65). London: Routledge.

Cudjoe, S. (1989). Jamaica Kincaid and the Modernist Project: An Interview. *Callaloo 39*, 396-411.

Davin, A. (1978). Imperialism and Motherhood. *History Workshop*, *5*(1), 9-65.

Garner, D. (1996). Jamaica Kincaid. The Salon Interview. *Salon* (April 13). https://www.salon.com/1996/01/13/kincaid_2

Hodge, M. (1970). *Crick Crack Monkey*. London: Heinemann.

Kincaid, J. (1983). *At the Bottom of the River*. New York: Farrar, Straus & Giroux.

Kincaid, J. (1985). *Annie John*. New York, NY: Plume.

Kincaid, J. (1990). *Lucy: A Novel*. New York, NY: Farrar, Straus & Giroux.

Kincaid, J. (1992). Biography of a Dress. *Grand Street*, *11*(3), 93-100.

Kincaid, J. (1995). *The Autobiography of My Mother*. New York, NY: Farrar, Straus & Giroux.

Kincaid, J. (1997). *My Brother*. New York, NY: Farrar, Straus & Giroux.

Kincaid, J. (2000). *My Garden (Book):*. New York, NY: Vintage. (First published 1999).

Kincaid, J. (2002). *Mr. Potter*. New York, NY: Farrar, Straus & Giroux.

Marshall, P. (1991). *Daughters*. New York, NY: Plume.

Perry, R. (1991). Colonizing the Breast: Sexuality and Maternity in Eighteenth-Century England. *Journal of the History of Sexuality*, *2*(2), 204-234.

Raiskin, J. (1996). *Snow on the Cane Fields: Women's Writing and Creole Subjectivity*. Minneapolis, MN: University of Minnesota Press.

Rody, C. (2000). *The Daughter's Return: African-American and Caribbean Women's Fictions of History.* Oxford: Oxford University Press.

Schiebinger, L. (2004). *Plants and Empire: Colonial Bioprospecting in the Atlantic World.* Cambridge, MA: Harvard University Press.

Snodgrass, M.E. (2008). *Jamaica Kincaid: A Literary Companion.* Jefferson, NC: McFarland & Co.

Spartacus, J. (2014). *Stratégies de survie chez Edwidge Danticat, Jamaica Kincaid et Toni Morrison* (Thèse de doctorat, Université Paul Valéry-Montpellier III).

Vorda, A. & Kincaid, J. (1991). An Interview with Jamaica Kincaid. *Mississippi Review, 20* (1/2), 7-26.

Walcott, D. (1992). The Star-Apple Kingdom. In *Le Royaume du fruit-étoile.* C. Malroux (Trans.). Belval, France: Circé. (Original work published 1979).

Walker, A. (1976). *Meridian.* New York, NY: Harcourt Brace Jovanovich.

Welter, B. (1966). The Cult of True Womanhood: 1820-1860. *American Quarterly, 18*(2), 151-174.

NINE

POSTCOLONIAL HAUNTINGS: GHOSTLY PRESENCE IN JAMAICA KINCAID'S *THE AUTOBIOGRAPHY OF MY MOTHER*

Simone A. James Alexander
Seton Hall University

Contact: Simone A. James Alexander, Seton Hall University
simone.alexander@shu.edu
To cite this article:
[Simone James Alexander. "Postcolonial Hauntings: Ghostly Presence in Jamaica Kincaid's *The Autobiography of My Mother.*" *Wagadu: A Journal of Transnational Women's and Gender Studies,* Summer 2018, vol. 19, pp. 106-129]

Abstract

The Autobiography of My Mother tells the story of loss, abandonment, survival, and resistance. This chapter explores the haunting or ghostly presence of both the living and the dead. The ghosts of slavery and colonialism haunt the character/s and the text; in retaliation, Xuela/Kincaid performs a "ghosting" by defying narrative conventions, by blurring the line between fiction, myth, biography, and autobiography.

Jamaica Kincaid's novel *The Autobiography of My Mother* tells the story of loss, abandonment, survival, and resistance. A creolized subject (daughter of a Carib mother and a half Scot, half-African father), the novel's protagonist, Xuela Claudette Richardson, embodies resistance, for she not only survives her mother's death, but she also survives her father's subsequent abandonment and several foster homes. Xuela's mother dies shortly after giving birth to her, leaving her in the care of her father who, in essence, abandons her as she is shuttled from foster home to foster home:

> When my mother died, leaving me a small child vulnerable to all the world, my father took me and placed me in the care of the same woman he paid to wash his clothes. It is possible that he emphasized the difference between the two bundles: one was his child, not his only child in the world but the only child he had with the only woman he had married so far; the other was his soiled clothes . . . That I was a burden to him, I know. (p. 4)

In the various foster homes, Xuela not only endures cruel treatment, but she also experiences sexual abuse at the hands of her foster parents, Jacques and Lise LaBatte. Ever resilient, Xuela outlives everyone, including the LaBattes, her husband, and her sister, living until the age of seventy. Xuela's traumatic birth resonates with the traumatic colonial history of the Caribbean, namely Dominica. Thus, Xuela's personal account of her life experiences echoes the collective narrative of loss, displacement, extinction, and exploitation of the island's history and its people. Critic Shu-li Chang (2004) reminds us that many women writers engage allegory as a narrative strategy: "In contemporary women's narratives, private traumas are almost always deployed as an allegory for collective traumas" (p. 106). While Xuela's mother's death symbolizes the extinction of the Carib people: "The Carib people had been defeated and then exterminated, thrown away like the weeds in the garden," as a creolized subject, Xuela's birth suggests the forging of a new nation, a Creolized community: "The African people had been defeated but had survived. When they looked at me, they saw only the Carib people. They were wrong . . ." (p. 16). Facing extinction and erasure, symbolized by the "x" in her name, Xuela registers her resistance.[ix] The simultaneous embodiment of loss and gain, the irruption/interruption of a life (of lives), of a cherished past: the loss of her mother and the loss of her Carib and African ancestors and culture are markers of Xuela's identity and existence. She captures this loss as follows: "This realization of loss and gain made me look backward and forward: at my beginning was this woman whose face I had never seen, but at my end was nothing, no one between me and the black room of the world" (p. 3). Xuela's birth coincides with the birth of the nation; both the nation and Xuela are born of resistance. Furthermore, Xuela's birth coincides with the birth of the novel, the creation of a "new" auto/biographical genre, a counter genre that resists narrative conventions. Xuela's autobiography doubles as her mother's biography; hence, Xuela is able to chronicle her life (and her mother's life) as an "other" and a "self." In writing as a "self" and an "other," Xuela assumes literary power over her personal narrative, her mother's history, and the island's history. The doubling/merging of the text renders indistinguishable the private/personal experiences from the collective experiences; it also shifts and blurs the boundaries/ definition of an auto/biography. In writing her autobiography, Xuela creates self and community; Xuela and her mother's story is the history of the island.

Kincaid's "disguise" of the novel as an autobiography engenders a kind of grafting that challenges the strict and inflexible definitions of the traditional autobiographical genre.[x] By definition, an autobiography is an account of a person's life written by that person. Kincaid's autobiography takes on hybrid characteristics, merging personal history with collective history, literary writing with myths, memories, and dreams. This genre-merging sets the text apart from the traditional male-centered and European autobiography.[xi] Kincaid's works resist easy classification, owing to her dismissal of European classifications of genres and refusal to accept "the purity of genres," resulting in a literary excavation of sorts that Jana Evans Braziel (2009) refers to as "autobiographical ambivalence" (p. 7). This literary excavation results in the toppling of traditional autobiography.

Arguing that the stretching of "autobiography's generic seams" is not new, "and can be likened to a restless and unmade bed [where] discursive, intellectual, and political practices can be remade," Alison Donnell (1999) stresses that the goal of *The Autobiography* is not "to define itself unproblematically as a piece of life-writing which takes either herself or her mother as its subject, but as a piece which addresses the multiple imbrications of self, m/other, and writing" (p. 124). While Donnell calls attention to the importance of women's autobiography, and particularly to Kincaid's "stretching" of the traditional autobiographical genre, her analysis is still limited to the personal: self, m/other, and writing. As discussed earlier, Xuela and her mother's personal experiences are linked to the collective, the Dominican community as a whole. Kincaid's blurring/splicing of subjects presents a formidable challenge to traditional autobiography; at the same time, it results in the undecipherability of determining to whom the auto/biography belongs: mother or daughter, or both mother and daughter. Or is it a tribute to the mother/land?[xii] This unknowability lends itself to "ghosting," an undecipherable haunting presence (as well as absence) that prompts Donnell to question if there is one or more than one auto/biographer of the text, and if it is "Kincaid's mother's auto/biography, then Kincaid is still present as the 'ghost' writer/biographer" (p. 127). Kincaid's "ghosting," her role as a ghostwriter is indisputable, evident in her repeated obsession with the mother (figure), her unrelenting portrayal of the mother-daughter relationship that is often fraught with tension. In *Annie John*, Kincaid portrays her imminent departure from Antigua as "ghosting," separation from her mother, ending the mother-daughter relationship. Similarly, the eponymous heroine of the novel, *Lucy*, refuses to read her mother's letter in an effort to silence her.[xiii] Kincaid is "ghosted" equally by her mother; in *Annie John*, Annie John Senior abruptly ends the practice of mother and daughter dressing alike, causing her daughter, Annie, great angst and separation anxiety.[xiv] In *Lucy*, convinced that she was writing the self, Kincaid finally concedes that she was writing the m/other:

> At the top of the page, I wrote my full name . . . At the sight of it many thoughts rushed through me, but I could write down only this: 'I wish I could love someone so much that I would die from it.' And then as I looked at this sentence a great wave of shame came over and I wept and wept that so much that the tears fell on the page and caused all the *words to become one big blur*. (*Lucy*, pp.163-4, italics mine)

True to its definition, a ghost or "ghosting" has inherent, interchangeable, nebulous attributes as both mother and daughter function as a ghost/writer; they both inhabit the body/space of a ghost/writer. Furthermore, the ghosts of slavery and colonialism both haunt and instruct their writing. Xuela muses:

> I knew the history of an array of people I would never meet. That in itself should not have kept me from knowing them; it was only that this history of peoples that I would never meet—Romans, Gauls, Saxons, Britons, the British people—had behind it a malicious intent: to make me feel humiliated, humbled, small. Once I had identified and accepted this malice directed at me, I became fascinated with this expression of vanity: the perfume of your own name and your own deeds is intoxicating, and it never causes you to feel

weary or exhausted; it is its own inspiration; it is its own renewal. (pp. 59-60)

Xuela's authoring, her recalling or "ghosting" of her dead mother, in this auto/biography, "can be seen as a type of ghost writing" (Shima, 2004, p. 63). Operating within the trope of "ghosting," this chapter explores the haunting or ghostly presence of both the living and the dead.[xv] In response, or more poignantly, in retaliation to the haunting occasioned by slavery and colonialism, Kincaid performs a "ghosting" of the autobiographical genre by defying narrative conventions, by blurring the line between fiction, myth, biography, and autobiography. For example, under the spell of colonialism, Ma Eunice, Xuela's first foster mother, is unable to distinguish fantasy from reality. Fascinated by,

> a picture painted on [a plate made of bone china], a picture of a wide-open field filled with grass and flowers in the most tender shades of yellow, pink, blue, and green; the sky had a sun in it that shone but did not burn bright . . . This picture was nothing but a field of grass and flowers on a sunny day, but it had an atmosphere of secret abundance, happiness, and tranquility; underneath it was written in gold letters the one word HEAVEN. Of course it was not a picture of heaven at all; it was a picture of the English countryside idealized . . . Eunice thought that this picture was a picture of heaven. (pp. 8-9)

This blurring-cum-doubling is a recurring theme in *The Autobiography*, and unsurprisingly, these blurred lines extend to the mother-daughter duo who functions as a "deathly double" that disrupts and derails colonizing forces. Ghosting speaks of simultaneous imitation and innovation; it registers hypervisibility and invisibility, hyperembodiment and disembodiment (Brown, 2015, p. 16).

Kincaid's work has been characterized as embracing numerous contradictions and *The Autobiography of My Mother* is no exception. Contradiction resides in the trope of blurring/doubling as Xuela's role as victim is interpreted as contradictory. As I discuss later, some critics are hesitant to identify Xuela as a victim of rape. Moreover, this contradiction resides in the title and the text, *The Autobiography of My Mother*. Accentuating the subversive theory that Kincaid engages routinely, Louis Simon (2005) writes: "The paradox of the title signals a subversion of language, a twisting and refuting of convention and conventional meaning that undergirds the entire text" (p. 31). Attempting to render decipherable what is often deemed undecipherable in Kincaid's writings, Daryl Dance surmises that despite the fact that Xuela bears Kincaid's own mother's last name (Richardson), she is more like Kincaid, the daughter, than the mother, Annie (p. 2). Misnomer is another narrative strategy that Kincaid adopts in *Autobiography*. Dance accordingly explains the contradictory title of the novel surmising that mother and daughter are one: "The fact that, in this novel, the mother and daughter are indeed one helps to explain the oft-noted incongruity of the title, for the 'autobiography' of her mother seems truly her own autobiography" (p. 2).

This blurring/merging between the mother and the daughter, between the present and the past, challenges linearity as it chronicles the chaos, the traumatic experiences endured by the characters: mother, daughter, and the island. We are duly reminded by Sandra Pouchet Paquet (1990) that non-linearity is "normative" as "West Indian autobiography is varied and complex" (p. 357). Furthermore, the non-linearity and complexity of *The Autobiography* manifests in the role of the predominantly female "authors": Kincaid, Xuela's mother, Xuela, and the island.[xvi] Kincaid's insertion of women into the text (read the national narrative) is not coincidental. Autobiography, for the most part, has been a male enterprise. Kincaid's seeming ease with challenging narrative conventions, encapsulates "[the] intense and creative struggle with the conventions of autobiography, and engage[s] directly with the social and political issues that have preoccupied West Indian culture and society"

(Paquet, p. 358). Kincaid's *The Autobiography* is also infused with the personal; as argued earlier, the personal mother-daughter relationship is politicized, metonymically representative of the mother/land.

Notably, Kincaid dedicates *The Autobiography* to the late Derek Walcott who, in his long autobiographical poem *Another Life,* stresses "a value other than autobiography" (Paquet, 1990, p. 358). Walcott himself confesses that in *Another Life* "he abandoned autobiography for elegy and intellectual history" (quoted in Paquet, p. 358). Walcott does not dismiss or devalue autobiography completely, for the poem is infused with autobiographical references. However, he does write a biography, so to speak, of his native West Indies. Kincaid's dedication is symbolic, for Walcott himself engages the bending of genres; this autobiographical poem comprised of over four thousand lines of verse is grouped into four parts. Walcott's rewriting and subversion of the poem to suit his post-colonial needs resonates with *The Autobiography* that gives Kincaid poetic license to fashion her novel to her own liking, to engender the proverbial intermarriage of the individual experience with the collective, colonial experience, and to personalize history and politics. Moreover, Walcott's *Another Life* navigates the political, personal and historical spheres, rendering an evocative portrayal of the West Indies, even as he writes an elegy of himself and man, humankind. Symbolically, *The Autobiography*, with its routinized breaking of conventions, is also an elegy. Kincaid/Xuela seeks, demands, and desires another life (a pun of the title of the poem), free from enslavement and colonial invasion. Furthermore, despite the innate tragedy of loss and abandonment, Xuela's mother is experiencing "another life," an afterlife: Xuela is also, albeit vicariously, as well as Dominica, in a postcolonial state. Illuminating how the brutality of colonialism has left the island's inhabitants in a zombified state, particularly Ma Eunice, who is debilitated by her inability to mother effectively, Xuela muses: "In a place like this, brutality is the only real inheritance and cruelty is sometimes the only thing freely given" (p. 5). The embodiment of the collective dilemma of a colonial Caribbean history (Paquet, p. 360), Xuela/her mother nevertheless exercises agency, for *The Autobiography* functions as a vehicle for self-exploration and self-articulation beyond the conventional/colonial text, beyond the dictates of patriarchy. As the representative voice of the vanquished, as both participant and witness, Xuela writes both herself and her mother into the narrative.

Despite her hypo-presence, Xuela's dead mother is hyper-present; her memory is kept alive by Xuela's constant return to, reimagining, and reconstruction of the past:

> For me history was not only the past: it was the past and it was also the present. I did not mind my defeat, I only minded that it had to last so long; I did not see the future and that is perhaps as it should be. And yet . . . and yet, it made me sad to know that I did not look straight ahead of me. I always looked back. (p.139).

Even as she acknowledges the importance of a collective history, Xuela's uncontrollable urge to "look back" is an act of remembering, of recollecting and re-visioning her dead mother. *The Autobiography* itself is a repeat, a re-vision of her mother's life/death. Xuela registers both her and her mother's ghostly presence, lending validity to the idea that haunting not only invokes but also evokes, "and like any other haunting, it has the desire to be seen" (Brown, 2015, p. 17). Morris's (2004) observation, "Jamaica Kincaid's writing thrives on bringing erasures back to life" (p. 954), echoes Veronica Marie Gregg's (2002) that establishes that the haunting presence manifests as a "form of spirit possession" and furthers this argument (p. 928). By looking back or gazing back onto the hauntings of the past, Xuela lends voice to Toni Morrison's (1988) classic phrase: "This is not a story to pass on" (p. 275). The decimation of the Carib people, the enslavement and subsequent colonization of black people should not be forgotten, must be remembered, must be memorialized for posterity.

The sporadic appearances of the dead mother, specifically, the appearance of her levitating heel, in Xuela's dreams,[xvii] the dead mother's refusal to be stilled—all contribute to the haunting, they "mark her presence as a haunted and haunting absence" (Gregg, p. 928). Xuela captures this horrific and melancholic void:

> I looked over my shoulder to see if someone was coming, as if I were expecting someone to come, and Ma Eunice would ask me what I was looking for, at first as a joke, but when, after a time, I did not stop doing it, she thought it meant I could see spirits. (p. 5)

Xuela's return is, in essence, a re-articulation of her mother's history, the island's history, and by default, her own history. Xuela manipulates her dreams, bringing back her mother from the dead: "I lay down to sleep and to dream of my mother—for I knew I would do that, I knew I would make myself do that, I needed to do that" (p. 31). In like manner, Xuela orchestrates her own resurrection through self-creation and bodily self-possession.

As a postcolonial subject and as an orphan, Xuela is forced to construct her identity via loss, destruction, and death of the mother/land.[xviii] Death, ironically, becomes the impetus for her existence, for her living. Since death is a destructive force, these constant images of the dead that serve as impetus for the living are precarious. The body's vulnerability finds resonance in the scarred and broken bodies of black women that repeat, that are passed down, in this case, from mother to daughter, making visible slavery's and colonialism's aftermath: the violence, the haunting, that has occasioned black women's vulnerability. The recurring and repeating visions of Xuela's mother engender continuity that resonates with what Kimberly Juanita Brown calls "the repeating body." Nevertheless, acknowledgement of the body's vulnerability empowers women to reclaim their bodies and sexual agency. Repetitions and duplications engender the reliving of memory, rendering those once invisible visible. Xuela, who bears the same name as her mother, gives voice to this duplication in the following quote:

> This account of my life has been an account of my
> mother's life as much as it has been an account of mine,
> and even so, again it is an account of the life of the
> children I did not have, as it is their account of me. In me
> is the voice I never heard, the face I never saw, the being
> I came from. In me are the voices that should have come
> out of me, the faces I never allowed to form, the eyes I
> never allowed to see me. This account is an account of
> the person who was never allowed to be and an account
> of the person I did not allow myself to become. (p. 227)

Addressing the injuries, the scars inflicted by colonialism, Xuela portrays how generations are affected by this invasion-cum-violation. Colonialism has created a nation (read an orphanage) of orphans. Marie-Claude Perrin-Chenour (2013) suggests that the repetitions testify "to an absence of evolution in spite of age and experience . . . mak[ing] it impossible for any [author, narrator and character] to become an integrated subject" (pp. 170-171). Repetitions, however, do not suggest stasis; in actuality, they offer "visual . . . and gendered iterations of the indelible memory of slavery" and colonization (Brown, p. 13). In the above quote, Xuela demonstrates how this memory has impacted both the mind and the body that are scarred indelibly.

The mother's ghostly presence both interrupts and engenders the flow of the narrative. Xuela's own birth is marked by interruption, the death of her mother who dies during childbirth. As noted earlier, this cycle of interruption becomes the defining moment of Xuela's existence as she asserts: "I came to feel that for my whole life I had been standing on a precipice" (p. 3). The "precipitous" existence is arguably the bane of Xuela's existence as death is the motivating factor of her life/living. She ironically forms relationships only after someone dies: "My brother dies. In death he became my brother" (p. 110). Debatably, she fuels her fall from grace by not heeding to the cautionary message meted out to the adolescent girl, and to girls in general, in Kincaid's short story "Girl" that demands that she practice and display proper feminine behavior: "Try to walk like a lady and not like the slut you are bent on becoming" (p. 3). Xuela's inability to live up to the ideals of womanhood is rendered palpable by the wife of Philip, the English doctor.[xix] Xuela recounts: "She was a lady, I was a woman, and this distinction for her was important; it allowed her to believe that I would not associate the ordinary, the everyday—a bowel movement, a cry of ecstasy—with her" (pp. 158-159). In contrast, Xuela embraces the "everyday" with fervor and passion, resulting in her exhibiting slut-like behavior: loving her body odor, overtly displaying passion and sexual desire, providing minute details of her sexual encounters: "Whatever I was told to hate I loved and loved the most. . . . Whatever about me caused offense, whatever was native to me, whatever I could not help and was not a moral failing—those things about me I loved with the fervor of the devoted" (pp. 32-33). Xuela's de-sanitization of her experience is a direct rejection of Victorian modes of decorum and decency. Thus, young women are walking a tightrope as they stand on the precipice of an endangered female sexuality. Both Xuela and her sister are expected to subscribe to and uphold the politics of respectability.

Questioning the politics of respectability, Kincaid interrogates patriarchal mandates that demand that women practice proper feminine behavior, meanwhile men's conduct remains unchecked. By sharing Xuela's age at the time of her first sexual encounter with Monsieur LaBatte, Kincaid calls attention to the fact that she is still under-age and therefore her violation constitutes statutory rape.[xx] Paradoxically, two paragraphs prior to her father's delivering her to Monsieur LaBatte, Xuela spoke fondly and proudly about her school days; in particular about how she excelled and surpassed expectations. The juxtaposition of her reminiscing about her school days and her "capture," her being transported to Jacques LaBatte's house, sheds light on her imminent loss of innocence.[xxi] Paradoxically, Xuela's father is a policeman, an enforcer of the law; his colonial authority finds representation in his policing of her body that culminates in his delivering her to her "jailer," Jacques. In a revealing scene, Xuela paid the price for defying her father's colonial authority. She challenges her father who claimed that he had no nails to give to the gravedigger, Lazarus, insisting that he had a full barrel:

> When Lazarus left, without the nails he had come for, without the nails he needed, my father grabbed me by the back of the neck of the dress I was wearing and dragged me through the house to the shed where he had the barrel of nails, and he pushed me facedown into the barrel of nails . . . This pain he was causing me, this suffocating me in a barrel of nails, was a true feeling of his. (p. 190)[xxii]

Therefore, Xuela has changed hands from one jailer to another. Her initial (geographic) dislocation that initiated her out-of-body experience: "I had never been to Roseau until that day" precedes her rape, her body estrangement (p. 60).

Forced by her surrogate mother, Lise, to have continued sexual relations with her surrogate father, Monsieur LaBatte, renders Xuela's rape more heinous. The LaBattes' presence calls attention to the elites/whites that dominated/haunted the planation economy. This imagery of slavery and forms of enslavement is prevalent, with Xuela revealing that she performs household chores in the "main house" before she leaves for school (p. 73). The violent act of rape mirrors the willful violence of Xuela's forced abortion: "If there was a child in me I could expel it through the sheer force of my will. I willed it out of me" (p. 81). Motherhood is defined by bodily rejections of childbearing. Xuela is not only forced into an illicit sexual affair with Monsieur LaBatte, but she is also used as a surrogate, as a vessel of reproduction. In other words, her body is used as capital. We are all too familiar with the fact that "Slave women's bodies, specifically their procreative capacity, were considered prime real estate capital and accordingly they were marketed for maximum profit" (Alexander, 2014, p. 75). Deborah Gray White (1999) reiterates that once it caught on that the "reproductive function of the female slave could yield a profit, the manipulation of procreative sexual relations became an integral part of the sexual exploitation of slaves" (p. 68).

Consequently, Xuela can be likened to her enslaved female ancestors, whose worth was determined and defined by their reproductive capacity. She later becomes fully aware of her exploitation by the husband-wife duo, but specifically by Lise. Complicit in patriarchal undertakings, Lise LaBatte does not see the need to examine her "contradictions of self, woman as oppressor" (Lorde, 1984, p. 130). Lise is more invested in putting forth her own agenda: her fervent desire to have a child by any means necessary and the attendant commodification of Xuela, who is not blinded to this fact: "She wants to make a gift of me to her husband; she wants to give me to him. . . . It was herself she wanted to save; it was me she wanted to consume" (p. 68, p. 94).[xxiii] In this regard, Lise is complicit in using the black female body as property, for profit. Lise's action is akin to female betrayal, despite reassuring Xuela that she should trust her and "make [her]self at home, to regard her as if she were my own mother, to feel safe whenever she was near" (p. 66). Lise, instead, opens up the historical wounds that find efficacy in the slave woman's body violation and subjugation.

Of her consumption, Xuela writes: "He took me to the room in which he counted his money, the money that was only some of the money he had. It was a dark room and so he kept a small lamp always lighted in it" (p. 70). Moreover, she occupied "a room that was attached to the kitchen; the kitchen was not a part of the house itself. . . . [She] slept in the room with the floor of dirt" (p. 67, p. 71).[xxiv] Her commodification is rendered most palpable when she reveals that her father knew Monsieur LaBatte "through financial arrangements they made with each other" (p. 60). Nevertheless, Xuela subverts the patriarchal manipulation by literally taking matters into her own hands when she performs an abortion. Invoking the historical practice of abortion that slave women performed, Xuela rejects her designation as propertied possession (Xuela's father, Monsieur LaBatte, and Lise LaBatte possessed her body through violence). Along these lines, she subverts the notion of the sexual "helplessness of the female slave, who was forced to be a breeding machine for the plantation" (Ormerod, p. 101).

Xuela's unequivocal refusal to become a designated mother (of the state) does not go unnoticed: "I had never had a mother, I had just recently refused to become one, and I knew then that this refusal would be complete. I would never become a mother, but that would not be the same as never bearing children. I would bear children, but I would never be a mother to them" (pp. 96-97). This distinction between being a mother and bearing children is of critical importance as it harkens back to female enslavement. Assigned the role of breeder, Xuela is deprived of her ability to mother and be/come a mother and thus unequivocally registers her challenge to this female (sexual) subjugation via the abortion. In her effort to thwart the LaBattes (the patriarchy) from profiting from her, Xuela engages a theory of subversion of sorts by liberating her unborn children:

> I would bear children, they would hang from me like fruit from a vine, but I would destroy them with the carelessness of a god. I would bear children in the morning, I would bathe them at noon in a water that came from myself, and I would eat them at night, swallowing them whole, all at once. (p. 97)

Suffice it to say, this form of self-fashioning finds representation in self-devouring, a form of narcissistic cannibalization. Furthermore, this motherly, liberatory act is not new. We are reminded of Toni Morrison's Sethe (1988), who, after being made aware of Schoolteacher's decision to claim her children, steadfastly articulated: "No notebook for my babies and no measuring string either" (p. 198). The haunting Xuela experiences by Lise claiming her unborn child is no less evocative or telling: "This vision she would have, of a child inside me, eventually in her arms, *hung in the air like a ghost*, something only the special could see. Not for every eye, it was for my eyes, but I would never see it, and it would *go away and come back*, this *ghost of me with a child inside me*. I turned my back to it; *my ears grew deaf* to it; *my heart would not beat*" (p. 77, emphasis mine). Whereas Xuela narrowly escapes death— "my heart would not beat"— by refusing to give birth to this unborn child, Edwidge Danticat's mother-protagonist, Martine Caco's parting words were: "I could not carry the baby" (p. 224) for she feared that her lover, Marc, "gave her the baby that's going to take [her] life away" (p. 190).[xxv] Both women are haunted by the recurring/repeating images of the unborn. Xuela's abortion, therefore, bears the imprint of an exorcism; similarly to Martine, she must exorcise the demon, Jacques's child, from within. Laying claim to black bodies replicates the slaveholding tradition of having control over women's bodies. Thus, Xuela has chosen to mother, to make herself: "No one observed and beheld me, I observed and beheld myself; the invisible current went out and it came back to me. I came to love myself in defiance, out of despair, because there was nothing else" (pp. 56-57); and in doing so, she reclaims her reproductive rights and sexual agency.

Xuela reconstructs the black female body not as a site of violence but as a site of resistance and resilience. The language of female resistance she invokes affords her the opportunity to claim ownership of her narrative of rape, and by extension, of her body. Celebrating her self-actualization, she writes: "Exhausted from the agony of expelling from my body a child I could not love and so did not want, I dreamed of *all the things that were mine*" (89, emphasis added). Self-devouring that carries the narcissistic imprint of self-loving is an act of self-actualization, also witnessed in Toni Morrison's *Sula* (1973). In response to her grandmother Eva Peace's advice that she "get married [because] you need to have some babies. It'll settle you," Sula brazenly interjects: "I don't want to make somebody else. I want to make myself" (p. 92). Like Sula, Xuela dismisses the procreative possibilities of female sexuality in favor of self-fashioning. In choosing self-articulation over patriarchal mothering, sex's primary purpose is recreational. Performing the abortion affords Xuela the ability to shed the cloak of victimization she earlier inhabited and don one that celebrates and promotes female agency. The termination of her pregnancy, therefore, is illustrative of resistance, rejecting further invasion/penetration of her body that in turn signals her refusal to procreate and to reproduce the nation, specifically, to replicate the traumatic colonial history of Dominica. Registering her disgust and disapproval of slavery and the subjugation of her people, Xuela chooses self-isolation over patriarchal subjugation: "My impulse is to the good, my good is to serve myself. I am not a people, I am not a nation. I only wish from time to time to make my actions be the actions of a people, to make my actions the actions of a nation" (p. 216). Yet, in this declaration, in this refutation of the nation, is the yearning/mourning to belong to a community.

Xuela expertly uses language to intercept her geographic —and body— destabilization. I reason that Xuela, similarly to her creator Kincaid, is a master-manipulator of language. This fact becomes manifest in the following passage: "He did not move away in embarrassment and I, too, did not run away in embarrassment. We held each other's gaze. I took off my clothes and he took off his clothes . . . When he was through with me and I with him . . ." (p. 70). The language used portrays unwavering self-assurance and intimates that Xuela initiated the sexual encounter and that she is Monsieur LaBatte's equal.[xxvi] However, this is far from the truth as we later find out that not only is it her first sexual experience, but that it also happens with an adult male who happens to be her father's age: "It was the first man I had ever seen unclothed and he surprised me. . . . I was *acting from a feeling I had*. The feeling I had, the instinct I was acting from, were *all new to me*. [Later] I washed the thin crust of blood that had dried between my legs and down the inside of my legs. I knew why it was there. I knew what had just happened to me" (p. 77, p. 70, p.72, emphasis added).[xxvii]

The language of victimization surfaces here, albeit momentarily, illuminating Xuela's false sense of security and her vulnerability, and shattering the protective wall of indifference she had built around herself. Brown cautions against refusing to acknowledge the body's vulnerability and slavery's and postcolonial violence. In a self-reflective moment, Xuela confesses that her "loss had made [her] vulnerable, hard, and helpless" and, shortly after being raped repeatedly, she confesses: "I could no longer be a child" (p. 4, p. 77). The phrase "I knew what had just happened to me" chronicles an out-of-body experience over which Xuela seemingly had no control, even as it gestures that Xuela is an unenthusiastic participant. Xuela inhabits a dual space: as spectator and participant. Despite Xuela's lack of enthusiasm, she nevertheless "validate[s] her own sexual pleasure within the gendered and racial oppressions which govern her life" (Schultheis, p. 8).[xxviii] It becomes self-evident that, "Sexual pleasure does not equal happiness nor transform Xuela into an adherent of the law of the father" (Schultheis, p. 26). As spectator, Xuela attempts to deflect the devouring colonial male gaze; she does so through the act of doubling, through (body) disassociation, that affords her the ability to transform the self or to assume another form or self: "A form of masking, doubling functions as a skillful strategy for survival that permits one to deal with brutality and harsh realities of life" (Alexander, 2014, p. 174). Protagonist Sophie Caco, of Edwidge Danticat's *Breath, Eyes Memory*, effectively doubles during sex.[xxix] Similarly to Sophie who receives temporary relief by doubling during sex, Xuela's disassociation from the physical act and the "actor" empowers her: "The body of a man is not what makes him desirable, it is what his body might make you feel when it touches you that is the thrill. . .. I was surprised at how unbeautiful he was all by himself . . . it was anticipation that kept me enthralled." (p. 70-71). Schultheis offers an explanation to this disassociation or critical distance: "Repeated experiences of displacement simultaneously produce the condition of self-reflexivity or critical distance that Xuela manifests so completely" (p. 15). This disassociation, in turn, engenders Jacques's disembodiment and subsequent disempowerment, as his virility and potency are fiercely interrogated: "His hands hanging at his side . . . the limp folds of flesh on his stomach" (p. 71). Hence, without the act, the actor, Jacques, is zombified, is rendered ghost-like. By focusing on the anticipated action rather than on the actor, Xuela creates an alternative space beyond the reach of patriarchal control. While Jacques LaBatte may have temporary access to her body, Xuela does not relinquish her mind and spirit.

Xuela appropriately invokes the language of violence to give voice to her body violation: "To each piercing he made inside me, I made a cry that was the same, a cry of sadness" (p. 71). "Physical pain," according to Elaine Scarry, "does not simply resist language but actively destroys it, bringing about an immediate reversion to a state anterior to language, to the sounds and cries a human being makes before language is learned" (p. 4.). Numbed by her experiences (both personal and historical): "Everything in my life, good or bad, to which I am inextricably bound is a source of pain" (p. 7), Xuela no longer succumbs to pain; instead, she is overcome by sadness. "Whatever pain achieves," Scarry surmises, "it achieves in part through its unsharability, and it ensures this unsharability through its resistance to language" (p. 4). When language fails Xuela, she captures her sexual exploitation via imagery that bears the imprint of physicality: His hands . . . not yet inside me . . . not yet opening my mouth wider to *place his tongue even deeper in my mouth* . . . the force of him inside me. A long sharp line of pain . . . each piercing that he made inside me" (p. 71, emphasis added). The near-suffocation that Xuela experiences earlier when her father forced her face into the barrel of nails surfaces here again as Jacques "place[s] his tongue even deeper in [her] mouth." These images of forced penetration encapsulate "what the female body undergoes during the physical act of rape . . . [in other words] representation of rape is thus achieved by highlighting the physical properties of sexual violence and revolves around the bodily reception of that violence" (Jean-Charles, 2009, p. 40). Xuela later admits that the sexual encounter had changed her: "I was not the same person I had been before" (p. 71).[xxx]

Xuela's manipulation of language has prompted some critics to dismiss that she was raped, and to disregard her bodily experiences of rape, arguing instead that she welcomed the sexual encounter and was an equal and willing participant. Daryl Dance, for example, claims:

> It is no exaggeration to say that often Kincaid (according to her writings) and the Kincaid characters (especially Lucy and Xuela) delight in acting the part of the 'slut' as Kincaid

> always delighted in doing the opposite of what her mother
> desired—and shocking everyone. (Dance, p. 70)[xxxi]

Because of her deliberate embrace of what one may deem a wanton and reckless sexuality, her unabashedly pleasuring herself and smelling herself in Jacques' presence, her refusing to wear underpants, her articulating both the pain and pleasure she experiences during sexual intercourse, Xuela is perceived as the active pursuer and seductress, becoming "the slut [she was] bent on becoming." Ann Cahill (2001) provides an accurate assessment of Xuela's ambivalence, of her assumed guilt and complicity: "Rape, itself, as a phenomenon, is profoundly multiple, deeply differentiated by a host of diverse and, at times, conflicting discourses. Yet, its possible meanings, while diverse, are always directly related to that complex interplay between the body and subjectivity" (p. 118). Acknowledging existing tensions embedded in the representation of rape, Régine Jean-Charles cautions against mythologizing rape survivors, against further victimization of the victims, noting that "The myths are about the context in which rape occurs, about the perpetrators of rape, about what a rape victim looks or acts like, and about how people respond to rape" (p. 44). She also challenges black women's dehumanization, the widespread belief that they are not victims of sexual violence. In spite of her bodily assaults, "out of this ambivalent social status comes [Xuela's] ability to claim instruments of power for herself" (Schultheis, p. 13). Therefore, Xuela's perceived reckless and wanton behavior is her articulating resistance to a colonial structure that aims to silence women literally and bodily. Her weapon of choice to combat female oppression is female sexual agency.

Xuela is not a consummate victim, and consequently her laying claim to her desires disrupts any simplistic reading of the power dynamics between her and Monsieur LaBatte (Schultheis, p. 24). At the same time, this blurring of the relationship does not construct Xuela as a hopeless and helpless victim. Actually, it allows her the space to articulate resistance; it aids in her self-reconstruction. Xuela exercises female agency by discursively manipulating the colonial language and by embracing her corporeality, by inhabiting her body (language). Unabashedly identifying with a "slut," using her own body as an instrument of pleasure and power, is Xuela's challenge to Victorian ideology of decency and propriety. In short, she refuses to be ashamed of her sexuality.

Fittingly, Xuela experiences a rebirth after confessing: "I could no longer be a child. . . . I was not the same person I had been before." This rebirth is appropriately heralded by torrential rain:

> It had rained during the night, a rain that was beyond torrential, and in the morning it did not stop, in the evening after the morning it did not stop; the rain did not stop for many, many days. It fell with such force and for such a long time that it appeared to have the ability to change the face and the destiny of the world. . . . I was in a *state of upheaval. I would not remain the same*, even I could see that; *the respectable*, the predictable—such was not to be my own destiny. (p. 73, emphasis mine)

The state of upheaval and disruption mirrors the complex birth process. Here, Xuela not only interrogates respectability politics—exposing the hypocrisy of the patriarchy that sanctions female morality, while men routinely engage in immoral acts—but she also laments her lost innocence. Chronicling her return to infancy, she writes:

> For the days and nights that the rain fell I could not keep to my routine: make my *own* breakfast, perform some household tasks in the main house in which Madame and Monsieur lived, then walk to my school . . . wash[. . .] my *own* clothes and generally tak[e] care of my *own* self. (p. 73, emphasis mine)

Thus, Xuela's helplessness that resonates with infancy is brought on by her rebirth that takes place in the very room with the dirt floor. The room is imitative of the womb, and Xuela's fetal-like position is epitomized by her inhabiting the "smaller version of the larger deluge": "I was standing in the middle of a smaller version of the larger deluge; it was coming through the roof of my room, which was made of tin" (p. 73). We witness a similar rebirth in *Annie John*, in the scene where young Annie, after suffering a breakdown because of a fractured relationship she has with her mother, is saved by her grandmother, Ma Chess.[xxxii] Whereas Ma Chess's presence facilitates new life for her granddaughter, Annie, Lise assumes the role of the "white savior." Well aware of Lise's patronization, Xuela articulates guardedly:

> She came *to rescue me*, she knew how I must *be suffering* in the wet. . . . She *could hear my suffering*, caused by this unexpected deluge, this unconscionable downpour; to be alone in it would be the *cause of much suffering* for me, she *could already hear me suffering* so." (p. 73, emphasis added)

Xuela's denigration is marked by Lise's infantilization of her, her portrayal of her as needy and dependent. Xuela's suffering is central to Lise's role as benevolent and wise liberator; as a suffering daughter, Xuela needs protection. Revealing the rampant pathologizing of black subjects, Xuela intimates that the colonizers deem suffering an innate characteristic of the colonized: "She could *already* hear me suffering so." Notwithstanding, she counters this narrative of black female victimhood: "But I was not making a sound at all, only the soft sighs of satisfaction remembered" (p. 74). This narrative of the suffering "other" even permeates Xuela's mother's relationship: "Placed outside a place where some nuns from France lived, they brought her up, baptized her a Christian, and demanded that she be a quiet, shy, *long-suffering, unquestioning, modest wishing-to-die-soon person*. She became such a person" (p. 199, emphasis mine). Interestingly, religion (Christianity), and suffering are coupled, presented as not-so-strange bedfellows.

Lending voice to this "white savior" myth, Guyanese poet Grace Nichols registers her disgust with the portrayal of black women as sufferers and as suffering. Verbally indicting those who are comfortable with black women being trapped "in a stranglehold of perpetual dependency and victimization" (Alexander, 2014, p. 128),[xxxiii] she quips that, to fuel the (master) narrative of black female victimhood, the "abused stereotype / already in their heads," they need to perpetuate "a mother-of-sufferer / trampled / oppressed" (Nichols, 1990, p. 285). Kincaid concurs that this narrative of black female oppression is preferred. Responding to the critics who were dissatisfied with and therefore critical of Lucy's identity-formation, she unapologetically retorts: "They wanted to hear about her oppression, and her racial discrimination;" adding that Lucy "is going to be disappointing for a small-minded reader" (Kincaid, 1992 p. 23).

Xuela's propertied status is magnified by Lise insisting that she wear her dress, which symbolically superimposes a colonial identity onto Xuela's own identity. This scene bears resonance with a similar scene in *Annie John* where the mother abruptly discontinues the practice of dressing alike with her daughter. The mother in *Annie John* expresses real fear of the consequences of her daughter's assuming or "wrongfully" appropriating an adult-woman's identity.[xxxiv] She is trying to deflect the male (gaze) from consuming and devouring her daughter. In other words, she is averting unsolicited male sexual advance. On the contrary, Lise's goal is to consume Xuela, to subsume her identity, transforming her into an object of male (and female) desire. Despite a perfect fit, Xuela chronicles her physical discomfiture: "The dress fit me perfectly, I felt most uncomfortable in it, I could not wait to remove it and put on my own clothes again" (p. 75). Lise's dress becomes a symbol of Xuela's haunting, her being hounded. Wearing Lise's dress speaks of erasure of an identity and the re-inscription of a colonial identity. Subsumed, Xuela becomes an apparition, ghost-like. Xuela is reminded that her own mother's identity was erased by the nun who found her outside the orphanage and arbitrarily added her name, Claudette Desvarieux, to Xuela's mother's original name. This superimposition of a colonial identity is redolent in the following passage: "[Lise] was *stitching me a garment from beautiful old cloths* she had saved from the different times in her life, the happy times, the sad times. It was a shroud made of memories" (pp. 77-78, emphasis added). This scene that reinforces Xuela's body consumption also signals Lise's domestication of her, which stands in for another form of colonization: "How she wished to weave me into its seams, its many seams. How hard she tried; but with each click of the thimble striking the needle, I made an escape. Her frustration and my satisfaction were in their own way palpable." (p. 78). Domestication furthermore bears the imprint of sexualization, as Lise forces Xuela to wear the dress to be desirable and sexually appealing to Jacques; she also conflates Xuela's sexualization and attendant subjugation. Lise's attempt to literally "graft" Xuela is intended to subsume her identity. Furthermore, this pastiche of sorts, this trope of weaving that resonates with the African American tradition of quilting, arguably is a form of cultural appropriation of black culture, a theft that ultimately is intended to culminate in Xuela's body theft. In a case of role reversal, whereas Xuela is expected to be Lise's (sexual) double, Lise is engaged in cultural appropriation. We witness a classic case of cultural appropriation, of theft, that plays out on a grander scale, as the British colonizing mission is in effect: "My sister wore a dress of white silk; it came from far away, it came from China, but it was said that she was married in English silk" (p. 127).

Xuela captures Lise's haunting presence, her desire to possess her in words: "My heart was not unmoved by the sight of Lise haunting the space of ground that stood between the house in which she lived and the small hut I occupied . . . I did not want the actual sight of Lise seeing me leave her to haunt me for the rest of my life" (pp. 93-4, p. 96). This haunting comes to a head when Lise shadows Xuela like a ghost as she awaits her return after the abortion.[xxxv] In mourning, Lise wears "a new black dress," as she plants "small bushes that bore white flowers" and then uproots and replaces them with lilies that "would eventually bear flowers the color of the inside of an orange" (p. 94). This rooting and uprooting of the flowering plants bears resemblance to Monsieur

LaBatte's planting his "seed" in Xuela, resulting in her pregnancy. Hence, both husband and wife engineered the haunting, the rape. The white flowers that symbolize purity and innocence, most likely Xuela's, are replaced by "flowers the color of the inside of an orange," that blood-like imagery attesting to innocence lost. Furthermore, the reddish, fleshy inside of the orange bears resemblance to the female genitalia. The white flowering plants that signify Xuela's burgeoning sexuality serve as a testimony to her subsequent deflowering. This scene of Lise planting flowers parallels a similar scene in which Philip also "had an obsessive interest in rearranging the landscape," prompting Xuela to conclude: "Gardening in the way of luxury . . . is an act of conquest" (p. 143). Thus, if Xuela's body is representative of the land, evoking Moira Ferguson's title "where the land meets the body," then Lise facilitates Xuela's disembodiment, her conquest.[xxxvi] This parallel scene of Lise's and Philip's (strikingly, his name evokes royalty, a member of the conquering class) obsession with planting (colonizing) speaks of Lise vying for supremacy, a fact that comes to light when Xuela observes that "she wanted to graft herself onto [Jacques], the way it's done with trees" (p. 76). Understandably, Lise wanted her and her husband to become one, congruent with the grafting of plants where tissues are joined to continue their growth together, and evocative of the matrimonial phrase: "a man shall . . . hold fast to his wife, and they shall become one."[xxxvii] However, Jacques "would not be had, he would not be contained" (p. 76).

Xuela later moves out of Lise's house into her own home; she also purchased the clothes of a recently deceased man— "I bought from his wife the garments of a man who had just died"— in which she went to work daily (p. 98). Completing the rebirth, she cuts off her plaits: "I cut off the two plaits of hair on my head; they fell to my feet looking like two headless serpents. I wrapped my almost hairless head in a piece of cloth. I did not look like a man, I did not look like a woman" (pp. 98-9,). The headless serpents, symbols of deceit, are representative of Lise and Xuela, both disempowered under the patriarchal regime. Thus, Xuela denounces female deception. Her new androgynous appearance is her refusal to be linked with treachery and deceit of/by women and with patriarchal control and violence of men. She frees both Lise and herself from the reigns of patriarchy and patriarchal designs of female sexuality. This de-gendering or de-sexualization—exemplified by the cutting off of her two plaits and her donning "masculine" attire—aids in deflecting the haunting and penetrating male gaze. Moreover, it provides relief, albeit temporarily, of the objectification of the female body as sexually desirable and as the vessel of procreation.[xxxviii] Kathryn Morris (2002) expounds on this line of reasoning: "The androgyny and her seclusion . . . allow a moment of transcendence from the realm of the social order where she exists as a woman, a fated, gendered subject" (p. 964). Xuela's bodily self-possession is complete when she removes herself from the patriarchal home in which Lise and Jacques reside.

Grafting or joining characterized as a horticultural technique is most commonly used in asexual propagation of plants. Thus, Xuela's rejection of surrogacy or othermothering registers her distaste and distrust of non-genetic relations, of artificiality. Further, this artificiality finds representation in the strained relationships she has with her adopted/surrogate mothers, resulting in her rejection of all forms of surrogacy, including becoming a surrogate mother for Lise. In designating Xuela as a vessel of reproduction, Lise participates in her asexualization, denying her sexual agency. Along similar lines, Lise's proverbial weaving of Xuela into the seams of her dress is akin to cloning as Lise attempts to make Xuela to her own liking/image. Drawing an interesting parallel, asexual or vegetative reproduction always produces plants that are identical to the parent. Xuela is keenly aware of this colonizing mission, which she avoids by refusing to reproduce, to become a "mother of the nation." This refusal is exemplary of a decolonizing act as she rejects the white nation as represented by the colonizers, Lise and Jacques LaBatte. In this way, Xuela simultaneously refuses to reproduce the nation and to feed the concept of the nation as family.

References

Alexander James, S. A. (2001). *Mother Imagery in the Novels of Afro-Caribbean Women*. Columbia, MO: University of Missouri Press.

Alexander James, S. A. (2015). *African Diasporic Women's Narratives: Politics of Resistance Survival, and Citizenship*. Gainesville, FL: University of Florida Press. (First published 2014).

Alexander James, S. A. (2017). Review of *In Search of Annie Drew: Jamaica Kincaid's Mother and Muse*, by Daryl Cumber Dance). *Journal of West Indian Literature* 25 (1), 113-117.

Braziel Evans, J. (2009). *Caribbean Genesis: Jamaica Kincaid and the Writing of the New Worlds*. Albany, NY: SUNY Press.

Brown, K.J. (2015). *The Repeating Body: Slavery's Visual Resonance in the Contemporary*. Durham, NC: Duke University Press.

Cahill, A J. (2001). *Rethinking Rape*. Ithaca, NY: Cornell University Press.

Chang, S.L. (2004). Daughterly Hauntings and Historical Traumas: Toni Morrison's *Beloved* and Jamaica Kincaid's *The Autobiography of My Mother*. *Concentric: Literary and Cultural Studies* 30 (2), 105-127.

Dance, D. C. (2016). *In Search of Annie Drew. Jamaica Kincaid's Mother and Muse.* Charlottesville, VA: University of Virginia Press.

Danticat, E. (1994). *Breath, Eyes, Memory.* London: Abacus.

Donnell, A. (1999). When Writing the Other is Being True to the Self: Jamaica Kincaid's *The Autobiography of My Mother.* In P. Polkey (Ed.), *Women's Lives into Print: The Theory, Practice and Writing of Feminist Auto/Biography* (pp. 123-136). New York, NY: St. Martin's.

Ferguson, M. (1994). *Jamaica Kincaid: Where the Land Meets the Body.* Charlottesville, VA: University of Virginia Press.

Gregg, V. M. (2002). How Jamaica Kincaid Writes the Autobiography of My Mother." *Callaloo* 25(3), 920-937.

Jean-Charles, R.M. (2009). Terre et Chair: Rape, Land and the Body in Gisèle Pineau's *Macadam Dreams.* In V. Theile & M. Drews (Eds.), *Reclaiming Home, Remembering Motherhood, Rewriting History: African American and Afro-Caribbean Women's Literature in the Twentieth Century* (pp. 29-50). Newcastle upon Tyne: Cambridge Scholars Publishing.

Kincaid, J. (2000). *At the Bottom of the River.* New York, NY: Plume. (First published 1978).

Kincaid, J. (1986). *Annie John.* New York, NY: Penguin. (First published 1983).

Kincaid, J. (1991). *Lucy.* New York, NY: Penguin Books.

Kincaid, J. (1992). Biography of a Dress. *Grand Street, 11*(3), 93-100.

Kincaid, J. (1996). *The Autobiography of My Mother.* New York, NY: Plume.

Kincaid, J. (1992). I Use a Cut and Slash Policy of Writing: Jamaica Kincaid Talks to Gerhard Dilger, *Wasafiri* 16, (autumn), 21-25.

Lorde, A. (1984). The Uses of Anger: Women Responding to Racism. In *Sister Outsider: Essays and Speeches* (pp 124-133). New York, NY: The Crossing Press.

Lorde, A. (1982). *Zami: A New Spelling of My Name.* New York, NY: The Crossing Press.

Morris, K.E. (2002). Jamaica Kincaid's Voracious Bodies: Engendering a Carib(bean) Woman. *Callaloo* 25(3), 954-968.

Morrison, T. (1988). *Beloved.* New York, NY: Penguin.

Morrison, T. (1973). *Sula.* New York, NY: Plume.

Nichols, G. (1990). The Battle with Language. In S. Cudjoe (Ed.), *Caribbean Women Writers: Essays from the First International Conference* (pp.283-89). Amherst, MA: Calaloux.

Ormerod, B. (1985). *An Introduction to the French Caribbean Novel.* London: Heinemann.

Paquet Pouchet, S. P. (1990). West Indian Autobiography. *Black American Literature Forum,* 24 (2), 357-374.

Perrin-Chenour, M.C. (2013). Jamaica Kincaid's Regressive Writing. *Recherches anglaises et nord-americaines,* 46, 163-172.

Scarry, E. (1985). *The Body in Pain: The Making and Unmaking of the World.* Oxford: Oxford University Press.

Schultheis, A. (2001). Family Matters in Jamaica Kincaid's *The Autobiography of My Mother." Jouvert: A Journal of Postcolonial Studies*

5(2) https://english.chass.ncsu.edu/jouvert/v5i2/con52.htm. Accessed 15 August 2017.

Shima, A. (2004). No Beginning, No End: The Legacy of Absence in Jamaica Kincaid's *The Autobiography of My Mother*. *Kunapipi* 26 (2), 61-73.

Simon, L. (2005). Triumphs of Ambivalence: Jamaica Kincaid's *The Autobiography of My Mother*. *Journal of Caribbean Literatures,* 4(1), 31-37.

Theile, V. & Drews, M. (Eds.) (2009). *Reclaiming Home, Remembering Motherhood, Rewriting History: African American and Afro-Caribbean Women's Literature in the Twentieth Century*. Newcastle upon Tyne: Cambridge Scholars Publishing.

White Gray, D. (1999). *Ar'n't I a Woman? Female Slaves in the Plantation South*. New York: W. W. Norton. (First published 1985).

Endnotes

i   This was the keynote address to the conference, "The Art and Craft of Grafting in Jamaica Kincaid's Works" held in Paris in May 19-20, 2017.

ii   *Global Trends* is the annual documentation of human migration and displacement published by UNHCR and available on their website.

iii   Both written with Monica Jardine from two angles, from the literary/cultural and the socio-economic.

iv   Interestingly, *The Grafter's Handbook* is currently published by Chelsea Green out of White River Junction, Vermont, the state Jamaica Kincaid long called home and where she keeps the garden readers have come to know from interviews, pieces in *The New Yorker* and *My Garden (Book):*. The manual was originally published in 1947 in London, England, just two years before the author's birth.

v   See Homi Bhabha, *The Location of Culture,* originally published in 1994, for more on the novel as a liminal space. For Bhabha, cultural objects like novels are inherently ambivalent spaces that may authorize or efface minority voices. This ambivalence is echoed in Kincaid's writing on the garden. For her, gardens are sites of pleasure, but also of discomfort and anxiety. They are spaces in which to map out the Caribbean, but also sites that are bound to the history and consequences of colonialism.

vi   Significantly, Dmitri means follower of Demeter.

vii   As Greene Benjamin asserts, Aunt Nancy is implicitly present in Paule Marshall's novel through weaving imagery that reconnects protagonist Avey Johnson to her personal and cultural history. *Praisesong for the Widow* makes several references to thin threads that stretch from Avey's navel and heart to others, creating community and bringing healing to Avey. See, for example, p. 160, pp. 190-191, pp. 249-250.

viii   "This island's mine, by Sycorax my mother,/ Which thou takest from me. When thou camest first/ Thou strokedst me and madest much of me, wouldst give me/ Water with berries in't, and teach me how/ To name the bigger light" (Act I, sc. 2).

ix   The symbol "x" is used to refer to a person, thing, and agency of unknown identity. See https://girvin.com/blog/the-symbolism-of-the-x/

x   This refashioning of the autobiographical genre is reminiscent of Audre Lorde who created a new literary genre that she titles "biomythography," a combination of history, myth, autobiography, and fiction. See Lorde's biomythography, *Zami: A New Spelling of My Name* (1982).

xi   In a powerful portrayal of resistance to traditional, patriarchal definition of an auto/biography, Kincaid titles her essay, "Biography of a Dress." (1992). In this essay, she chronicles her mother and her ambivalent relationship, and their relationship to the m/otherland.

xii   Kincaid is known for blurring the lines between mother, motherland, and mothercountry. For a more detailed analysis of this "trichotomy," see Alexander, *Mother Imagery in the Novels of Afro-Caribbean Women*.
      Kincaid arguably uses personification here, another narrative strategy that de-normalizes the normative autobiography.

xiii Although Kincaid has claimed that her novels are not autobiographical, my reading of these novels is determined by their autobiographical content. My argument, therefore, is that Kincaid's work is semi-autobiographical.

xiv   "Ghosting," in the form of doubling or haunting/shadowing the m/other, is rendered palpable in the title of the book, *Annie John*. The mother and daughter are doubles, Annie John Senior and Annie John Junior. Moreover, this appropriation and subversion of the patriarchal practice where, traditionally, boys are given the names of their fathers engenders a "ghosting" of the colonial practice.

xv   While the term "ghostly presence" is oxymoronic, as the presence of a ghost suggests (bodily) absence, it is befitting the pervasive contradictions and ambiguities of the text.

xvi   I am referring to the island as female/feminine because often nations are referred to in the female gender. My use of personification is also in keeping with Kincaid's adoption and adaptation of figures of speech.

xvii Xuela does not characterize these appearances as dreams or dream-like, but they are real and function as part of her daily routine.
      The appearance of only the mother's heel exemplifies Kincaid's use of metonym whereby part is representative of the whole.

xviii The postcolonial subject is orphaned in essence, for s/he is deprived of a mother/land.

xix   Xuela married Philip after his wife passed. She is quick to point out that she is not a substitute lover: "But this is not to say that I took her place" (p. 160). Paradoxically, Philip's power is diminished (they moved to the mountains to live among the Caribs). His conquest is reduced to him cataloguing books: "He now busied himself with the dead, arranging, disarranging, rearranging the books on his shelf. . . . He now lived in a world in which he could not speak the language" (p. 224).

xx   The age of consent in Dominica is 16 years old. The age of consent is the minimum age at which an individual is considered legally old enough to consent to participation in sexual activity. Individuals aged 15 or younger in Dominica are not legally able to consent to sexual activity, and such activity may result in prosecution for statutory rape or the equivalent local law. Dominica statutory rape law is violated when an individual has consensual sexual intercourse with a person between ages 14 and 16. For additional details, see https://www.ageofconsent.net/world/dominica.

My interchangeable use of rape, sexual exploitation, sexual violence, sexual experience, sexual encounter, sex relation is not intended to diminish the severity of the act/action, or to dismiss the manipulation of procreative sexual relations, but rather to lend to the ease of analysis and the narrative flow.

xxi   This "delivery" arguably is akin to human trafficking, engendered by geographic dis-, re-location. Similar to those trafficked, Xuela is psychologically and emotionally vulnerable, she is experiencing economic hardship, resulting in a nomadic existence, and she lacks a social safety net.

xxii The phallic-like nails that are the source of Xuela's pain and near-suffocation also have the ability to pierce her. Later, we witness a parallel scene at play in which she lends voice to the pain and piercing she experiences during her rape.

xxiii   This scene is reminiscent of slave masters "gifting" their wives slave children. Specifically, when a slaver's child "was born or married, he or she might receive the gift of a black attendant." See http://www.pbs.org/wnet/slavery/experience/family/history2.html .

In the contemporary situation, Xuela arguably is "sold" as a sex slave, for her relationship with Monsieur LaBatte is purely sexual. He never functions as her surrogate father.

xxiv   This room with the floor of dirt that is attached to the kitchen is exemplary of Xuela's class position in this household, and in the nation of Dominica as a whole. She belongs to the class of the vanquished. Her marginal status/role is evocative of the marginalization of her people, Africans and Caribs.

xxv   Refusing to reproduce the nation, Martine takes her unborn child by killing herself. Here, the act of protest has a doubling effect: abortion and infanticide. For a more detailed discussion, see Alexander, *African Diasporic Women's Narratives: Politics of Resistance, Survival, and Citizenship*.

Similarly to Xuela, Martine also complained about being unable to breathe (p. 191).

xxvi   Xuela calls attention to class hierarchy: "Monsieur LaBatte was already a rich man, richer than my father. He had better connections; he had not wasted his time marrying a poor Carib woman for love" (p. 67). Like his predecessors, Monsieur LaBatte is on a colonizing mission.

xxvii   Xuela intimates that Jacques LaBatte was a "repeat offender": While she was "acting from instinct, he was behaving in a way he knew well" (p. 77). Like Xuela's father who left Xuela's face stuck in the barrel of nails to enjoy the tranquility of the sea, Jacques is unencumbered by acts of violence.

xxviii   Xuela's ambivalence brings to the fore the precipice (a sign of the uncertain and the unpredictable) that she is constantly fearful of falling off. She speaks of the simultaneous pain and pleasure of sex "a current of pure pleasure," "ache of pleasure" (p. 71, 72).

xxix   To avoid being "tested," a symbolic rape of sorts, where a mother inserts her index finger into her daughter's vagina to ensure that her hymen is intact, Sophie engenders her own self-rape by ramming a pestle into her vagina.

xxx   Monsieur LaBatte's dominion and domination of Xuela is most tangible in the scene, after the rape, when Xuela observes his coins, "their sides turned heads up; they bore the face of a king" (71). This observation is followed by her sharing with the readers that her room has a dirt floor.

xxxi   In a recent review of Dance's book, *In Search of Annie Drew: Jamaica Kincaid's Mother and Muse*, I questioned Dance's interpretation of Kincaid's perceived wanton sexual behavior (Alexander 2017).

xxxii   This scene is analyzed in detail in my book (Alexander 2001, 69-72). Notwithstanding, Annie describes her fetal-like position in the following manner: "I would lie on my side, curled up like a little comma, and Ma Chess would lie next to me, curled up like a bigger comma, into which I fit" (p. 125-6).

xxxiii   For a detailed analysis of Nichols's poems, see Alexander (2014).

xxxiv   This appropriation resonates with the Caribbean trope of being "forced-ripe,' that is, becoming a woman prematurely, before one's "time."

xxxv   This shadowing, reminiscent of policing, suggests that the LaBattes perpetuate the policing role of Xuela's father and function as her jailers.

xxxvi   Xuela elaborates that Philip's obsession with the growing of flowering plants did not wane because "these plants d[id] exactly what he wanted them to do" (p. 143).

xxxvii   http://biblehub.com/esv/genesis/2.htm .

xxxviii Of noted significance, Xuela does not only purchase a pair of trousers and an old cotton shirt from the wife of the man who has recently died, she also purchases his "old nankeen drawers" (p. 98).